The 2010 PRAIRIE GARDEN

WESTERN CANADA'S ONLY GARDENING ANNUAL

WRITTEN BY & FOR WESTERN GARDENERS

A non-profit publication dedicated to the advancement of horticulture in the Prairie Provinces

71st Annual Edition

2010 Theme
Annuals & Biennials

Special 32 page Colour Section

General Gardening Information

ISBN 978-0-9736849-5-7

Published by:
The Prairie Garden Committee
P.O. Box 517
WINNIPEG, MB R3C 2J3

Co-Chairs . . . . Ed Czarnecki & Colleen Zacharias
Editor . . . . Richard Denesiuk
Guest Editor . . . . Carla Hrycyna
Treasurer . . . . Jean Pomo
Secretary . . . . Linda Pearn
Associate Editors . . . . Reg Curle, Ed Czarnecki , Valerie Denesiuk,
Stefan Fediuk, Phil Graham, Jim Kohut,
Susanne Olver, Linda Pearn, Jean Pomo, Philip Ronald,
Terry Smith, Kevin Twomey, Sandy Venton,
Frances Wershler & Colleen Zacharias

Price: $12.00 per copy
Special quantity prices available to horticultural societies,
garden clubs, commercial outlets, etc.
For inquiries and order form, see page 184.

Printed in Canada by:
Kromar Printing Ltd.

Acknowledgements

The Prairie Garden is a non-profit publication. We appreciate support from a number of companies who share our interest in prairie horticulture. The following companies provided financial assistance toward this edition of *The Prairie Garden*. Their help is crucial in bringing this book to you at minimum cost as production and distribution costs rise annually. We welcome and thank the companies who provided sponsorship this year. Readers may contact them at the addresses below and can recognize their products by their logos, found on the back cover and on our Web site:

www.theprairiegarden.ca

Barkman Concrete Ltd. - 909 Gateway Rd., Winnipeg, MB R2K 3L1
Ph: 204-667-3310 website: barkmanconcrete.com,
e-mail: wpgsales@barkmanconcrete.com

Friends of the Assiniboine Park Conservatory - 15 Conservatory
Drive, Winnipeg, MB R3P 2N5 Ph: 204-837-4324 website:
friendsconservatory.com, e-mail: friendsconservatory@mts.net

Jeffries Nurseries Ltd. - P.O. Box 402, Portage la Prairie, MB R1N 3B7
Ph: 204-857-5288 website: jeffriesnurseries.com, e-mail: jeffnurs@mts.net

Kackenhoff Nurseries Ltd. - P.O. Box 2000, St. Norbert, MB R3V 1L4
Ph: 204-269-1377

The Lily Nook - P.O. Box 846, Neepawa, MB R0J 1H0 Ph. 204-476-3225
website: lilynook.mb.ca, e-mail: info@lilynook.mb.ca

Lindenberg Seeds Limited - 803 Princess Ave., Brandon, MB R7A 0P5
Ph: 204-727-0575 website: lindenbergseeds.mb.ca, e-mail:
lindenbergr@lindenbergseeds.mb.ca

Prairie Horticulture Certificate Program The University of Manitoba,
Winnipeg, MB R3T 2N2 Ph: 1-888-216-7011, ext. 6037,
website: umanitoba.ca/coned/mpcp/phc, e-mail" w_otto@umanitoba.ca

Schriemer's Home & Garden Showplace - 1505 Molson St., Winnipeg,
MB R2G 3S6 Ph: 204-668-8357 website: schriemers.ca, e-mail: info@
schriemers.ca

Shelmerdine Garden Center Ltd. - 7800 Roblin Boulevard, Winnipeg, MB
R4H 1B6 Ph: 204-895-7203, website: shelmerdine.com, email: info@
shelmerdine.com

St. Mary's Nursery & Garden Centre Ltd. - 2901 St. Mary's
Rd., Winnipeg, MB R2N 4A6 Ph: 204-255-7353 website:
stmarysnurseryandgardencentre.ca, e-mail: stmgardn@mts.net

T&T Seeds - P.O. Box 1710, Winnipeg, MB R3C 3P6 Ph: 204-895-9962
website: ttseeds.com, e-mail: garden@ttseeds.com

The 2010 Prairie Garden Table of Contents

Front cover Osteospermum 'Orange Symphony'
(photo courtesy of www.provenwinners.com)
Photo credits are in parentheses on all photos

Guest Editorial
by Carla Hyrcyna

Carla Hrycyna is president and co-owner of St. Mary's Nursery & Garden Centre Ltd. Fifteen years of retail greenhouse management blends nicely with her natural flair for landscape design. Carla is also the primary grower for St. Mary's Nursery instilling the "sown and grown by St. Mary's" philosophy.

Over the past quarter century, gardening has undergone significant change. Gone are the days of simplistic landscape design when a city garden may have consisted of only a select number and type of annuals. The focus on residential curb appeal through the use of annuals was virtually non-existent nor did the garden exist as a typical venue for a recreational pastime. Displays of large colourful gardens were generally restricted to the formal grounds of large institutions or paired with vegetable gardens in rural communities.

Gardening in the 21st Century has gained interest not only as an enjoyable pastime but also as a growing movement to beautify and enhance life in communities and urban centres. The desire to create luxurious gardens with all elements of plant material has exploded. The knowledge and creativity to achieve this goal has also evolved with a wealth of resource material available to today's home gardener. The 2010 issue of The Prairie Garden explores the theme of Annuals and Biennials and will enhance the reader's understanding of the diverse selections available at local garden centres.

Thirty years ago The Prairie Garden featured the topic of annuals which today takes on a new meaning. Gardeners across the prairies continue to explore beyond the boundaries of the traditional definition of annuals. The interesting result is that some of the plant selections and their uses described in this edition of The Prairie Garden may not conform precisely to what has been past practice.

"The Miracle and Suspense of Seeds" by Dr. Carla Zelmer begins by portraying the process of seeding in easy to understand steps. The stage is then set with landscape designer Rosie Chard's article "Designing with Annuals" which provides practical uses for garden favourites including dahlias, begonias, fuchsias, gladiolas and impatiens. The reader will be introduced to new ways to enjoy old favourites combined with an appreciation for exciting new introductions and color selections.

Geranium varieties, for example, have expanded from zonal (bedding) varieties to ivies, scented and Regal, including novelties such as Vancouver Centennial and the intriguing Crystal Palace Gem. Petunias have undergone dramatic change, as described in John Van Beveren's article, with many new varieties on the horizon. Older floribundas and grandifloras are now combined with mini petunias

(Piccola Series), Calibrachoa, Wave, and Cascade. This scenario is the same for many other annual varieties.

Increased demand for the use of plant material in an 'annual' capacity has driven gardeners to experiment with the use of perennials in their plantings. Not only do we use perennials hardy to our zones for both beds and containers, but the more adventurous of us are exploring the use of tender perennials for the impact of a single season of display.

A garden can be planted for all seasons. Annuals, although limited to a single growing season, play an integral role in adding color, texture and drama to the garden. Whereas the harsh prairie winter dictates to a large extent the plant choices available to gardeners, the choice of annuals is almost endless. Within these pages you will find inspiration to seek out the many selections now available at your local garden centre. Readers will enjoy the 32 pages of stunning photos and anticipate the opportunity that springtime brings to plant some of their favourites.

With this edition, The Prairie Garden is proud to continue in its commitment to contribute the most up to date information on plants available to the prairie gardener. "The science and history of plants teach us, but it is the wisdom of a true gardener that inspires us." 🦐

An Editorial Note
by Richard Denesiuk

Gardening in zones 2–3 definitely has it challenges, and rewards – but thank goodness for the instant gratification of colourful annuals! With our short gardening season, it's fantastic to come back from the garden centre with trays of exotic annuals that can spice up our gardens immediately. A technical definition of annuals (that you will read elsewhere in this edition) makes much of what we prairie gardeners consider to be annuals, actually not annuals, but rather perennials. However, in zone 2–3 there is considerable latitude we allow ourselves to enjoy our gardening season.

This 71st edition of The Prairie Garden has a great selection of articles that are informative, practical and inspiring. Growing from seed is a challenge that has been considered only for the 'serious' gardener, however, you will soon learn what a rewarding experience it can be. You will get some insight as how to choose annuals that will do well in your particular micro-climate, learn about some of the lesser-known and 'wow-factor'

annuals available and how to employ them in the gardenscape, as well as some great articles in our General article section.

I'd like to thank our guest editor, Carla Hrycyna, for her guidance with this year's theme of annuals as well as her contribution of articles. The Prairie Garden committee has done a very fair consideration of all articles and continues to ensure the high quality publication we have grown to expect. 🦐

How to Plant Your Garden

First, you come to The Garden alone,
while the dew is still on the roses

For the garden of your daily living,

Plant Three Rows of Peas:
1. Peace of mind
2. Peace of heart
3. Peace of soul

Plant Four Rows of Squash:
1. Squash gossip
2. Squash indifference
3. Squash grumbling
4. Squash selfishness

Plant Four Rows of Lettuce:
1. Lettuce be faithful
2. Lettuce be kind
3. Lettuce be patient
4. Lettuce really love one another

No Garden is Without Turnips:
1. Turnip for meetings
2. Turnip for service
3. Turnip to help one another

To Conclude Our Garden We Must Have Thyme:
1. Thyme for each other
2.. Thyme for family
3. Thyme for friends

Water freely with patience and cultivate with love.
There is much fruit in your garden,
because you reap what you sow.

-- Author Unknown

What Are Annual And Biennial Plants?

by Elizabeth Punter

Elizabeth Punter is a botanist and Assistant Curator of the University of Manitoba Herbarium. When she isn't out exploring, she enjoys gardening in Winnipeg.

An annual plant completes its life cycle in a single growing season. The seed germinates in the spring or early summer, grows roots and shoots, then flowers and produces seeds. Seeds are shed and the plant dies at the end of the growing season. Only the dormant seed bridges the gap between one growing season and another. So each year, annual species are dependent on successful re-establishment from seed. The dormant seeds will only germinate under appropriate conditions of soil temperature and moisture. Flowering is controlled by day length.

Annuals represent about 11% of the total native plant species in Canada. In the northern hemisphere, the number of annual species decreases from the equator northwards, probably due to the shorter growing season at higher latitudes. Annuals make up about 30% of total species of plants in deserts and semi-arid regions at lower latitudes. Many of the annuals used in prairie region gardens are native to other geographic regions

of the world with climates or growing seasons quite different from the northern prairies. They can be grown in prairie gardens because the seed can be started indoors or in greenhouses early in the year and planted out in the garden when the weather is frost-free.

Annuals include: Petunia, Zinnia, and Marigold from South America, Impatiens from Asia and Africa, and Lobelia from South Africa. Corn (Americas), Lettuce (Asia), Peas (Asia), Green beans (South America), and Watermelon (Africa) are annuals used as vegetables or fruit. Many common garden weeds are annuals: Chickweed (*Stellaria media*), Shepherd's-purse (*Capsella bursa-pastoris*) and Lamb's-quarters (*Chenopodium album*).

A biennial plant's life cycle spans two growing seasons. In the first year, the seed germinates to produce a root system and a very short stem, barely

Life cycle of an annual: (l-r) seed → germination → growth → immature plant → flowering → seed set and death.

above soil level, with a rosette of leaves. In the second season, the stem elongates, producing flowers, fruits and seeds. After the seeds are dispersed, the plant dies. The root produced in the first season is often a tap root in which food reserves are stored for growth in the following season. The rosette of most biennials requires exposure to the low temperatures of winter to induce flowering in the second season. Biennials for the flower garden include Honesty (Eurasian), some cultivars of Hollyhocks (China), Forget-me-nots (Europe), Siberian Wallflower (North America), Iceland poppy (northwestern North America, Greenland and Eurasia), and Sweet William (Eurasia). Many plants used as vegetables are truly biennials but are harvested as annuals. The first year leaves of Parsley (Europe) are used as a herb. Tap roots of carrots and parsnips produced in the first season of growth are used as vegetables. Some cultivars of Beetroot (Europe) are biennials. The swollen root is used as a vegetable, as are the young first year's leaves of Swiss Chard (same species as Beetroot, but a different cultivar). Rutabaga (Europe) is also a biennial in which the enlarged base of the leafy stem is eaten as a vegetable.

Some plants have a lifecycle that is halfway between annual and biennial. These are winter annuals whose seeds germinate in the fall to form a leafy rosette at soil level. In the following spring or early summer, they produce a leafy stem, then flowers, fruits and seeds. After the seeds are shed, the plant dies. These plants are considered annuals because their life cycle is completed within one calendar year but is spread over two growing seasons.

A number of tender perennials, especially vegetables, are also grown in prairie gardens as annuals (Tomato, Peppers).

Annuals and biennials add another dimension to the garden. Their flowers add colour to the garden while their leaves, fruits and seeds provide food with a little international flavour!

Life cycle of a biennial (clockwise starting at first year): seed → germination → growth, immature plant → rosette → (over-winter) 2nd year rosette → flowering and seed set → seed dispersal and death of adult plant.

(start cycle first year)

(over-winter and start of second year)

(Fran Wershler)

Using Perennials As Annuals
by Jim Kohut

Jim Kohut is the President and one of the founders of Northscaping (www.northscaping.com), the leading resource and community website for northern homeowners, landscapers and gardeners living in hardiness zones 1-5. He is also a regular writer for the Info Zone resource on the site. He can be contacted at grapevine@northscaping.com.

Perennials are plants that are able to survive the winter to regrow and repeat their performance in subsequent years, whereas annuals live for exactly one growing season, relying on seed to produce the next generation of plants each year. Because of these defining characteristics, annuals and perennials tend to be stereotyped into specific applications in the garden. We use annuals in containers and planters and to fill spaces in our gardens with waves of colour for immediate impact, while perennials typically comprise the backbone of a mixed border.

However, the differences between the two are often more subtle than you might think. Many of the "annuals" we grow on the prairies are in fact perennials in warmer climates, and it's our cold winters that limit their tenure in our gardens. As such, the issue might be better framed as one of disposability; an annual is a plant you expect to discard after a single growing season, while you presume a perennial will persevere for a number of years. Cost isn't much of a limiting factor nowadays; with so many perennials being "mass produced" they are often more affordable than the latest designer annuals.

What would motivate a gardener to use a perennial in the place of an annual? Many of the trendy perennials are not reliably hardy on the Prairies, but hardiness is no longer a consideration if they're being used as annuals. Many of the newer perennials offer an impressive range of enduring foliage colours that can complement the sometimes overpowering flowers of many annuals. Some perennials are even more vigorous than annuals, particularly in hot and dry or shady locations. Or, you might just desire to use your favourite perennial in a container or planter!

Not all perennials are candidates for use as annuals. Look for fast-growing and vigorous selections that will hit the ground running, because they have exactly one year to do their thing. Some of the most vigorous perennials tend to spread around the garden by seed or runners; the "culls" make excellent candidates for containers! On the other hand, many perennials don't like to be disturbed or are very slow growing; you can safely rule these out. If flowers are the primary ornamental feature, look for varieties that will bloom vigorously in the first year of planting. Don't overlook perennials with bold foliage colours, textures and forms, as these will endure over the entire season.

Perennials usually take longer to establish from seed or cuttings, so consider purchasing older and larger plants for use as annuals. Be careful to adjust the recommendations on the plant labels as required. Recommended spacing between plants is usually based on mature plant sizes, so the spacing will need to be tighter for first-year fullness. A more aggressive fertilizing regimen is also advisable in most cases, and you don't need to stop fertilizing in mid-summer if you're not concerned about winter survival.

Finally, there are pros and cons you should consider when using perennials as annuals. The majority of perennials will have shorter periods of bloom than their annual counterparts, so plan accordingly. On the other hand, if you dig your perennials into the garden for the winter, there's at least some chance that they will survive into the spring, while there's little to no chance of this with annuals.

Here are a few perennials to consider using as annuals;

Trailing
- *Lysimachia nummularia* 'Aurea' (golden creeping jenny)
- *Vinca minor* (periwinkle) cvs.
- *Lamium maculatum* cvs.

Upright
- *Salvia nemorosa* (perennial sage) cvs.
- *Veronica spicata* (spike speedwell) cvs.
- *Gaura lindheimeri*

Mounded
- *Geranium sanguineum* (bloody cranesbill)
- *Chrysanthemum* x *morifolium* (garden mum) cvs.
- *Monarda* (beebalm) cvs.

Long-blooming flowers
- *Rudbeckia hirta* (Black-Eyed Susan) cvs.
- *Gaillardia* x *grandiflora* (blanket flower) cvs.
- *Achillea* x *millefolium* (yarrow) cvs.

Showy foliage
- *Heuchera* (coralbells) cvs.
- *Pulmonaria* (lungwort) cvs.
- *Lysimachia punctata* 'Alexander' and 'Golden Alexander'
- *Artemisia* (wormwood) cvs.

See page 90 for pictures

The Miracle and Suspense of Seeds
by Carla Zelmer

*Dr Carla Zelmer is a Research Associate in the
Department of Plant Science, University of Manitoba.*

Since childhood, I have always planted seeds in the spring. I used to think that maybe it had something to do with descending from farmers long ago, but now I'm not so sure. I think that I plant because I simply can't resist doing so. The act of planting a seed is such an optimistic gesture, such a powerful statement about the end of winter and about the harvest to come that I am unable to stop myself.

I am captivated by the magic and mystery of seeds. During one spring of my childhood, I had taken over my mother's small corner garden, just a tiny quadrant of a circle surrounded by stones. I defended my right to this small patch, because I wanted to have my own garden. There was not a lot of garden space in our yard, so this bed was hotly contested. Finally, my mother allowed me to have the garden, on the condition that I let her plant one seed in it. That sounded like a reasonable compromise. After all, what could be the harm in just one seed? My mother happily planted her one zucchini seed, and rather than being upset at the re-

Fig. 1

sulting huge plant, I was hooked even further by the incredible potential contained in just one seed.

That potential has a long history. In the earliest land plants, dust-like spores were commonly produced, and many of the earth's plants, such as mosses and ferns, still do reproduce by spores. The spores actually represent a different generation of the plant's life cycle, and the tiny plants produced by the germination of spores have only one task – reproduction. Spores from a fern produce what looks like a miniscule crop of lettuce, and once these tiny plants reproduce by producing eggs and sperms cells, a new fern (the generation that we recognize as ferns) is formed. The reproductive generation is very delicate, and so they are restricted to living in consistently moist habitats.

A major innovation of the vegetable world was the development of seeds. The spores producing the egg cells were retained in the body of the spore-bearing plant, and the spores that would ultimately produce the sperms cells were sent abroad to find them, in the form of pollen.

Once the pollen grains landed on the stigma of the appropriate flower, their pollen tubes released to the egg the two sperm nuclei they had produced. A new embryonic plant was formed from the union of egg and sperm, and developed in the protective environment of the spore-bearing plant. Once the embryo was provisioned with oil, protein and other essentials for its nutrition and wrapped in a protective seed coat, it was released to the world as a seed. Since the reproductive generation was no longer vulnerable to drying out, plants could now grow and reproduce in the harshest climates, and their durable seeds could disperse far and wide. The seeds themselves were dry, light and easily dispersed, provisioned with necessary nutrients, well protected against the elements, and their embryos in a state of nearly suspended animation were capable of extended dormancy. Skip forward several million years, and you will see how these characteristics eventually lead to another great innovation: the mail order seed catalogue!

Why grow your plants from seed? The local nurseries are doing a great job supplying seedlings for our gardens, but it is a tough business with tight margins, and so generally they need to grow more common plants with wide appeal, ones that will sell well. There are, however, so many interesting plants that don't fit that description. They are uncommon, odd, interesting, surprising, sometimes even a little ugly in a cute sort of way. They

may never be offered for sale in your neighbourhood, but that doesn't mean that you can't grow them. Somewhere out there, someone is selling these seeds. Carnivorous plants, bonsai specimens, annuals, perennials, trees and shrubs, almost any plant can be grown from seed. Seeds can be economical too. Dozens, sometimes hundreds of plants can be raised from a package of seed that costs less than a 6-cell pack of nursery-grown plantlets of the same kind. In many cases, you can also save the seeds from your own plants to sow again the following spring. More than anything, though, raising plants from seed is fun. It's only fun when it works, however, so here's some information I hope will help you to successfully raise your plants from seeds.

Seeds contain everything needed to ensure the germination and growth of a small plant. A seed comprises an embryonic plant, a food reserve, all the biological machinery required for the building of the plant body and the release of energy from the food stores, as well as a seed coat that protects them from damage, predation and sometimes moisture. Seeds also have the ability to sense when the environmental requirements for germination are met. For each species, these requirements vary, but may include threshold temperatures, moisture availability, light (or the absence of it), day length and others. Remember, they are well equipped to wait, so they can remain dormant until these needs, however complex, are met. When you decide to plant seeds, you need to know what these requirements are. Seed packets are often the best source of this information.

Once you've planted your seeds, you may wonder what they are doing 'in there' or if anything will come of your efforts. Rest assured that if you have done your homework and given them what they need, they will be preparing to germinate. To keep the embryos dormant and healthy during the wait, seeds dry down to only a fraction of the moisture content of a growing plant. They shut down nonessential life functions, and disassemble some of the machinery that is not being used, such as chlorophyll, but they keep the pieces close at hand. Germination starts with the seeds 'imbibing' water. Most seeds will swell to several time their dry dimensions (Fig. 1). Once the water content is restored, they can begin to reassemble some of the biological machinery they will need to grow. This process can take some time, but varies greatly from species to species. Once the process begins, it is irreversible. This means that if you let germinating seeds dry out again, they will die, not become dormant again. Consistent moisture is essential at this stage!

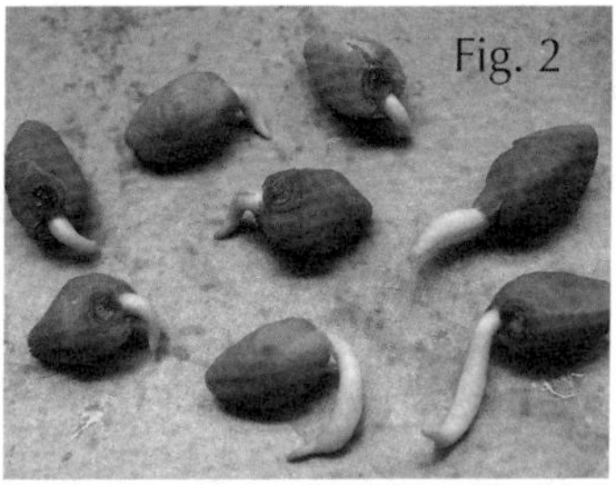

The first outward sign of germination is the appearance of the radicle ('little root'), which grows downward to become the seedling's root system (Fig. 2). Once this anchors the seedling in the ground, the seedling is poised to hoist its solar collectors up to the sunlight. Just as you might use your shoulder rather than your head to throw open a stuck door, the seedling uses a bend in its stem (the 'hypocotyl arch') to break through the soil surface (Fig. 3). You've probably seen beans coming through the soil this way. Seeds planted in heavy or very fibrous soil can sometimes fail to emerge because they cannot lift their seed leaves up through the soil. Fine vermiculite or a germination mix to cover the seeds is often recommended for this reason. A seed planted too deep will run out of energy to do this before reaching the soil surface. Seeds that are too old may also fail at this stage, because they have used up their germination energy on life processes while they waited for germination. In most cases, germination goes smoothly and the seedling leaves, or cotyledons, are raised to the sun and their surfaces exposed for the first time. The cotyledons expand rapidly, using the sun's energy to produce sugars for growth (Fig. 4). This is the start of the seedling plant's independence. Cotyledons, while distinctive for plant families, usually do not resemble

Fig. 2

the true leaves of the plant. The first true leaves make their appearance a short while later from between the paired cotyledons of most flowering annuals. Onions, grasses, lilies and other plants have single cotyledons at germination. This is a major division of the plant kingdom. Those plants that have two cotyledons are known as dicotyledons, those with only one as monocotyledons. This seemingly simple split reveals large differences in the world of seed plants, correlating with such things as which will be killed by the lawn herbicide 2,4-D, and which can be most easily grown from cuttings.

The tissues of the young plant are very soft and undefended by waxy layers or hairs, so, at this stage, they are naturally very vulnerable to many kinds of predators. Seedlings of plants grown indoors often fall prey to damping-off fungi. These are common soil fungi that thrive in overly wet soil in stagnant air. Seedlings attacked by these fungi suddenly topple over at the soil level, and a whole cohort of seedlings can die off quite rapidly. The use of sterilized potting or germination soil mixes for seed sowing helps to prevent this, as does aeration and proper watering (moist, not soggy). Uncover your seeding trays at the first sign of germination if you have used a plastic lid for humidity. A commercial fun-

gicide for damping off can be used successfully to rescue seedlings at the early stages of damping off.

What if they don't germinate? After a reasonable period of time has passed (check germination times on the package), poke around in the soil to see if you can find a seed. Press the seed between your fingers. A soft seed that oozes opaque fluid is dead and is being consumed by soil microorganisms. Often this indicates that the soil was too wet, or the seed was old and dead when planted. If the seed is hard and intact, it can mean that germination has not yet occurred. Make sure that you provided all the germination clues (temperature, light etc.) that were recommended on the package. Another possibility is that the seed has a waterproof seed coat, and so has not imbibed water to start the germination process.

Fig. 3

Check the size of the seeds to see if they are noticeably larger than the original dry seeds. Some, like sweet peas, moon flowers and some morning glories can use a little help. Scuff up the surface of the seeds with a nail file and try again. Is the plant you are growing a perennial, perhaps a species native to cooler or drier areas? Such plants often have extra dormancy-breaking requirements so that the seeds wait to grow until the spring after the seeds were released. Growing in the fall, or at the start of a dry season would limit their survival. Seeds of our native plants often need 6 weeks of cool moist incubation (a process called stratification) to signal the return of spring. This can be easily accomplished by folding the seeds in moist (not wet!) paper towelling and popping the towel into a sealable sandwich bag. Label it, put it in your fridge and forget about it until the note on your calendar tells you it is time to pull it out. Plant the seeds as usual after stratification. Cold moist stratification is most common for our native plants, but those from other areas may require more than one cold incubation after a warming period or other complex conditions. Plants from fire-adapted grasslands and forests may even require the presence of a component of smoke to germinate, but these are by far the minority of plants.

Once your seedlings have emerged, good lighting is your key to success. As soon as the seedlings emerge, they respond to the intensity of the available light. If the light level is too low, they will stretch upward in search of stronger light. In nature, this allows the seedlings to rise above objects that are shading them, such as fallen leaves or neighbouring plants, to reach their place in the sun. If you do not provide intense light indoors, and for a long enough time period each day, this important response will produce spindly, weak plants that fall over when watered. Since few of us can meet the light requirements to produce stocky, short seedlings with the natural light from our windows, supplemental lighting should be considered absolutely necessary. This does not have to be expensive or elaborate. A couple of shoplight florescent fixtures wired with a plug, a few bricks and an optional powerbar and timer is all that it takes. Set the shoplights side by side on the bricks so that the bulbs are no more than four to six inches above the tallest seedling. One cool white and one warm white bulb per fixture ensures the right light spectrum. As the plants grow, additional bricks can be added to raise the bulbs to the proper height. Your lights can stay on for 16 hours per day, which is conveniently controlled by the timer.

Once the first set of true leaves has unfurled under the lights, move the seedlings to larger pots. Gently lever each one out and support it if necessary by holding on to a cotyledon—NOT the stem! In seedlings, the stem is a delicate system of food and water-carrying conduits. Damage to the stem can result in the death of the seedling. Tuck it into the new pot of moist soil at the same level it was growing in the original container.

Now that your seedlings have the light they need to fuel their growth and the room to grow, they are going to need more nutrient supplies for 'body building'. Check your bag of potting soil. Some will come with the convenience of added fertilizer, which is often adequate for one to six weeks. In other cases, your potting soil will contain no added fertilizers, so you may add a liquid fertilizer once every two weeks to your regular watering schedule. What kind should you use? There are many different kinds, and some are more specific to certain types of plants, but generally you can get away with a simple balanced fertilizer with micronutrients. This means that three of the major plants nutrients (nitrogen, phosphorous and potassium) are

Fig. 4

available in equal amounts (e.g. 20-20-20), and the micronutrients (such as iron, copper and boron) that are required in smaller amounts, although still essential, are present as well. This will keep your plants green and healthy until the spring. Once they are planted out, I highly recommend the use of organic fertilizers instead of synthetic ones. Your local nursery should be able to point you in the right direction.

For houseplants, the hard work is done, and it is just a matter of ensuring that the developing plants are kept healthy and green by simply meeting their needs – water in an appropriate

amount, light of a high enough intensity and the occasional dose of fertilizer. A well aerated place in your house may also be appreciated. If the plants are intended for outside, you need to enrol them in 'plant bootcamp', a program of physical conditioning to toughen them up for the real world. This process takes a week or two, and it involves placing them outdoors for increasingly longer periods of time in a sheltered spot out of doors. At first they need to be protected from direct sunlight and strong winds, but they will adapt to the new conditions by thickening their stems, producing protective waxes on their leaf surfaces and adapting to the drying conditions that come with the wind. In time, a reduction of water and fertilizer will help them produce strong bodies that can withstand the rigours of garden life. Please have some patience and compassion for your seedlings during this process. How long would it take you in an exercise 'bootcamp' to get into shape? Soon they will be blooming beautifully in your garden. They just need a little time.

At summer's end, when they have fully matured and dried down, many of them will have left behind something precious and miraculous for you: seeds! See if you can resist planting them next spring. 🦃

How to Read a Seed Packet
by Carla Hrycyna

Beginning in January, the garden centre's phone starts ringing; a fair percentage of these calls relate to the question … "Are the seeds in yet?" In late winter, gardeners are anxious to get their plans in motion, which 'new seed' to buy, or which 'favourite seed' to choose for the upcoming planting year.

As we seek out our favourite seed packets from among the vast selections, it is difficult to resist picking a new variety or two. Seed displays can easily hold up to a hundred or more varieties. How do you choose? Is it the colourful packaging, the unique flower, or the thought of creating a new vegetable/ herb garden that draws our attention to purchase the packet? Recently, we are seeing more packaging touting their 'Organic' origins. I like many others, are tempted by all the colourful varieties, and even after many years of seeding plants for the garden centre, I still find selections amazing.

Reading a seed packet can be an adventure in itself. Usually we first seek out the seed selections by flowers, herbs, perennials, or vegetables, and secondly, by variety. Avid gardeners know the varieties they seek, including the growing conditions and the growth habit of these plants by heart. It is the new gardener, or the experienced gardener seeking a new item, that is driven to seek out information on the seed packet they have just selected.

Colourful seed packets measuring only 10 x 13 cm (4 x 5 in) relay to us some information valuable to the success of the plants growth. These packets generally give the guidelines for planting. Packets list seeding depth and spacing for row plantings. Some seed packets make the spacing issue simple for you by supplying the seed in a 'tape' format. Basically, the seed is matted to a paper tape that holds the seed in uniform spacing for row planting. Usually, smaller seeded varieties like carrots, beets, radishes, portulaca and snapdragons are made into seed tapes, reducing the number of plants and time needed to 'thin out' them out.

Cosmos mix
(Carla Hrycyna)

For most packets, the instructions specifically state seeding times for two methods of seeding. The first method would be to seed indoors for early maturity, and secondly, to seed directly in the garden. Specific time frames are usually listed for these methods.

Items listed, such as days to germination and days to maturity, are important facts. This is the part of plant biology that amazes me—different seeds germinate at different time frames, and mature at different rates as well. This is important, especially if seeding plants indoors. For example, marigolds will germinate in two–three days, whereas cleome and Datura take longer, 14 – 21 days. We just mentioned two different plants, yet, it is not unusual for one genus (i.e. marigolds, which have numerous varieties) to have different sowing dates and germination times. For example, the Marigold 'Crush' Series should be seeded by early March, whereas Marigold 'Safari Series' and 'Disco Series' do best seeded in April.

Planting location is generally noted in terms of full sun, part sun or shade. Included are specifications on the seed's growth in height, and comments such as "stunning in the garden" (taken directly from the Ontario Seed Company's Sweet Peas 'Royal Pink' packet sitting on my desk).

When browsing over your packet, it is helpful when seed quantity is stated. Some packets, depending on seed variety, will contain numerous seeds (petunias for example) while others may only contain a limited number, as with impatiens. Knowing the seed count will enable you to get the correct amount of seed you require. Oftentimes there is less seed count, as well as lower germination in lower valued packaging.

Seed size listed on the packaging is sometimes depicted by drawings showing 'actual size'. I have found this handy, specifically when seeking seed that can be handled easily by a young child or by someone that does not have the fine dexterity needed to handle very small seed (here too, the 'seed tape' packages come in handy). Packages listing 'vacuum seal or foiled for freshness' usually contain a 'seed sachet' inside an outer decorative seed packet, making it hard to actually guess how many seeds are within.

I don't know about you, but just investigating the aspects of a seed packet has inspired me to look more closely at the seed racks. Be advised though, that the more you look, the more you will be tempted to try a variety you have not grown before. As I write this, my personal list has grown, with Cosmos being at the top of my list. Cosmos 'Gazebo Red' and Cosmos 'Polidor' are outstanding, or at least the glossy adorned packages tease me with colourful blooms. No worries here, I know Cosmos is a beautiful flower! ❧

Seeding Annuals Outside
by Susanne Olver and Linda Pearn

Susanne Olver is a retired greenhouse supervisor from the Dept of Botany, University of Manitoba. Linda Pearn is retired from Plant Science Dept, Faculty of Agricultural and Food Sciences.

All avid gardeners dream of a beautiful garden with lots of flowers, constantly in bloom. Gone are the days when people planted a few petunias or geraniums in front of their houses and were satisfied.

Perennials are a lovely choice, but their flowering period is, for most species, restricted to a week or two. Therefore, you need a sequence of plant species to provide constant bloom. Nice as they are, we want flowers all through our short summers.

The obvious choice, then, are annuals. They come in a profusion of colours, shapes and sizes. Annuals can be obtained in two different ways:

1. Bedding plants – seedlings which have been started indoors and transplanted into individual cells of a pack or pots.
2. Seeded outside directly into the ground in the desired location.

In this article, we will deal with outdoor seeding exclusively.

Advantages or Benefits of direct seeding
• There are fewer steps to go through because the seeds are planted in the place where they will grow and bloom.

• The plants do not suffer any shock or set back from being transplanted.
• Seeds are much less expensive than already started plants. Dependent upon species, a seed package may contain up to 100 seeds for approximately two dollars while bedding plants may cost $3.00 and up for just six plants.

Disadvantages of Direct Seeding
• If some seeds don't germinate, there will be blank spots in your garden.
• Seeds with a long germination period and/or a long maturity time (from germination to flowering) would not have enough time from seeding to produce flowers before frost.

Planning for this undertaking is crucial, and can be done early in the year, when the gardeners' thumbs are starting to itch, but the outdoors is still covered by snow. Armed with a cup of tea, pencil and paper, and a seed catalogue or two, the gardener can start dreaming. First, a sketch of the garden or the flower beds should be made, indicating what should go where. Next, make a list of what can be seeded out, and when. The seeding time can vary, depending on the weather, and the plant variety. Also, one should try to find out how many seeds are in a package. Then comes the purchase of all the treasures.

A good nursery will have its seed packages out early. If ordering by catalogue, one should order early to avoid the disappointment of desired seeds being out of stock.

Preparation of soil

In preparation for seeding, once the ground is open, the planting area should be worked to a fine tilth. If the ground is heavy, peat moss can be added to lighten it up. Manure should be avoided. The peat should be moistened before using—dry peat repels water, moist peat has a great water holding capacity.

Seeding & Thinning

At the right time, the seeds should be scattered, and, if possible, not be crowded. If the seeds are very fine, they should be pressed lightly into the soil; if they are a bit bigger, lightly covered, and deeper if they are much bigger. To cover the seeds, finely sifted soil should be used—big lumps make it hard for the little seedlings to push through. Seeds that are planted too deep may suffocate, but, too close to the surface they might dry out. One trick to avoid drying out is to cover the area with damp sheets of newspaper, which should be regularly checked, and removed as soon as the seedlings are coming up.

Where seedlings are crowded, some plants should be thinned out (removed) to the specified spacing on the seed package. Plants that crowd each other will not grow properly. Try to avoid disturbing the roots of the plants you want to remain in situ. Often these extra seedlings can be transplanted to fill in areas where germination was poor. A thin spatula will help to dig them out with their roots. It is good to cover them for a day or two, until they have taken hold.

Conclusion

This issue of The Prairie garden will give you a list, (page 121) indicating seeding times, both indoor and out. Indoor seeding will give you larger plants to plant out, and earlier blooms, but indoor space is often limited. Annuals can bring colour to your garden with very little effort or expense.

Protect your bulbs from pests

It's no fun to find your newly planted bulbs on the soil surface after you have planted them. Squirrels and other critters will dig and snack on tulip bulbs, but they hate daffodils (narcissus). One way to foil their efforts is to plant these two kinds of bulbs together. Plant the tulips 8inches deep, add some soil and bone meal and plant the daff bulbs at 6 inches deep. Squirrels dig around in freshly turned earth to hide peanuts or to find the tulips, but when the find the narcissus bulb they will be discouraged and move on.

Dancing Queens of the Garden:
A Spotlight on Annuals
by Marilyn Dudek

Marilyn is a Master Gardener who enjoys garden designing. She serves on the Board of the Friends of the Assiniboine Park Conservatory and also works part-time at the Information Desk at Schriemer's Home & Garden Showplace.

One of the first questions you might ask yourself when planning a garden is what plants would give you pleasure. Would you prefer the 'Mamma Mias' with their hot, boisterous, fun colours or the more serene, calming colours of Swan Lake? Annuals can offer you a range of summer moods. Annuals mean that they last one year (*annum*) or for Prairie gardeners, one summer. Floriferous annual plants are bred to give the garden continual bloom. They strive to grow, flower profusely, set seed, and die. This process may sound rather sad, but in doing so, the annuals successfully accomplish their task: to continue their lives through the seeds they produce. I shall discuss many aspects of the annual garden: colour, flower, leaf size and shape, quantities, variation of genus, and vertical interest. While there are some general rules about how to choose and plant annuals, I think it is also important to break these rules at times, so I shall show you how to follow and when to break gardening rules.

The first question to ask yourself is which dance or colour theme do you want to perform or plant? Ask yourself, what mood do you want to feel? Do you want to follow current colour trends? What colour is your house exterior? Is there a colour scheme you have seen that appeals to you? For instance, almost all gardeners who visit the famous English gardens of Vita Sackville-West's Sissinghurst, will soon plant a white garden. This monochromatic garden is so beautiful and impressive with its variety of flowers and leaf colour, texture, size and shape, that people cannot help but be smitten by it

A monochromatic all pink garden
(Proven Winners)

and then want to replicate it. White can be a bright, but also a calming, peaceful colour, and as a bonus, it glows as a night garden.

When deciding on your colour scheme, it is imperative to choose no more than three colours. To quote Vancouver's Southlands nurseryman, Thomas Hobbs, "anything more than three colours begins to look like a pizza." The quantity of the same colour and variety of annuals planted in one spot is another factor in realizing a desired effect. Planting with a minimum of six of the identical plants together gives the garden the strongest eye view, which can be a chorus line kick of colour. A good tool for the gardener is a colour wheel. With it, you can decide whether you want to use combinations of single colours (monochromatic); warm colours (yellows, reds, oranges); cool colours (blues, purples); opposite colours which bring dramatic contrast (purple and yellow, blue and orange); or harmonizing colours which are next to one another on the colour wheel. Also, consider using dark leaves or flower colours, which give depth to your garden. One of the most fabulous colour gardens I have visited was Sandra and Norrie Pope's Hadspen Garden in Somerset, England. Granted it was a larger area than many of us could ever dream of gardening, but one of the many garden rooms was planted in a circle that encompassed the entire colour wheel and included both annuals and perennials. A garden such as this one requires immense foresight and planning, but it demonstrates the extent to which one can strive and imagine.

One of the most important lessons that this garden taught me was to forget about one of the "rules" of planting, which claims that you should use tall plants in the background and short plants in the foreground. It was here that I learned to walk with tall plants brushing my shoulders, causing me to stop and peer through them to see what was planted behind. Slowing down and enjoying really looking at a garden is an ultimate treat to oneself or a compliment from a visitor in your

Nicotiana sylvestris
(Nóra)

garden. Hence, in my garden, I too brush shoulders with the tall *Nicotiana sylvestris*, *N. langsdorffii*, *Helianthus annus* (sunflower), *Cleome*, *Antirrhinum majus* (snapdragons), *Amaranthus caudatus*, *A. cruentus*, *A. perfecta* and *Verbena bonariensis*.

For the most successful annual summer garden the gardener must know the positions of sun and shade in their planting areas. All plants survive on certain inbred traits with light requirements as one of the most important. To plant a shade lover in full sun would cause a quick shrivelling of leaves and an early demise. Sun lovers planted in shade may survive a bit longer, but they would eventually elongate striving for light and/or rot in the more moist conditions of the shade soil. In order to bloom, flowering sun lovers need long periods of sunshine.

When planning your annual plant selection, always consider the leaf size and shape. Through different shapes and sizes the garden texture becomes more tapestry-like and less static. This combination introduces many varieties of beautiful and impressive non-flowering annuals. Look to the immense variety of coleus now available with many more new introductions every year. Recently they have been available for only shade gardens but now many varieties can be planted in the sun to realize an even greater potential, which is a wonderful boon to the gardener who loves

to incorporate the electric exotic colours bred into *Coleus* 'Life Lime'; *C.* 'Royal Glissade'; *C.* 'Sedona'; *C.* 'Dipt in Wine'. Vegetables too, can compliment the annual garden through their assortment of colour, leaf shapes, size, and occasional bloom. Wonderful examples are *Beta vulgaris'* Northern Lights' (swiss chard); *Lactuca sativa* 'Lollo Rossa' (red curly loose leaf lettuce); *Capsicum annuum* "Black Pearl' (a pepper species); and *Brassica oleracea* 'Redbor' or 'Winterbor' (kale). *Cynara cardunculus* (Cardoon/Artichoke) becomes an excellent exclamation point. That these vegetables are both beautiful and edible makes them even more desirable for annual gardens.

Consideration should be given to vertical plants which take the eye up in the garden and offer more variety in planting. Vines are one answer, and their varieties increase yearly. Tropical vines, possibly invasive in their 'native' growing areas, are ideal for Prairie gardeners to plant as annuals. Many of these vines have trumpet-shaped flowers which attract hummingbirds. A number of vines can be grown inside from seed, which can be started six to eight weeks before the last frost. Seed catalogues introduce new varieties before nurseries and, hence, are excellent sources for the gardener who desires new introductions. Some seed favourites of mine are *Vigna Caracalla* (Corkscrew vine); *Convolvulaceae* 'Mina lobada'; *Ipomoea* x *multifida* (Cardinal Climber); *Asarina scandens* 'Jewel Mixed'; *Cobaea scandens* (Cup and Saucer vine); and *Tropaeolum peregrinum* (Canary Bird vine). Not to be forgotten are the ever popular *Lablab purpureus* (Hyacinth bean); *Nasturtium majus* (climbing nasturtium); *Lathyrus odoratus* (sweet pea); *Basella rubra* (climbing spinach); and *Phaseolus coccineus* (scarlet runner bean).

With these tips in mind, you are now ready to visit the nursery. Remember the ideas, thoughts, quantities, and the requirements of the plants you will choose. As previously mentioned, floriferous annuals strive to bloom and set seed. Gardeners now have to 'trick' them into continuing their colourful dance through our gardens all summer. Trick one is to choose the bushiest healthiest non-blooming plants in the nursery. If that is not possible, immediately after planting, cut off the blooms. These are two of the most difficult rules to follow for gardeners, but they reward us immensely. We have now 'tricked' them into believing that they have to continually bloom, as long as we continue to deadhead them (cutting or pinching off the spent flowers). Because of this fast growing lifespan we must continue this process of deadheading. This process of pinching plants may be where the idea of a gardener's green thumb originated. Of course, to every rule there is an exception. Hybridizers have now bred plants that 'self clean,' which means that no deadheading is needed. Look for these or similar words on plant tags. Examples are *Calibrachoa*, *Impatiens*, *Begonia semperflorens* (wax begonias), *Scaevola* (fan flowers), and *Torenia* (Wishbone flowers).

Dancing into the garden with plants in hand we are now ready to plant. If time warrants, try to leave newly-purchased plants to acclimatize outside, keeping in mind that a sheltered location is ideal. Remember that the more soil that is covered with plants, the less room there is for weeds, which means less tilling and more summer relaxation for you. Plant roots should be moist before placing them in the ground. After planting in a proper-sized hole and filling it, water the plants well with a transplanter product mixed into the water. In approximately the first week, more care is needed; watering well lessens the shock of moving plants from a sheltered greenhouse to the often-harsh reality of the outdoor climate.

Just as one might dance to a piece of music in order to reflect a mood, so gardeners are artists who create moods from the blank canvasses of their yards. Gardeners can bring harmony, joy, and peace to their gardens, giving way to their musical spirit and freedom to feel those senses. Dance your hearts and souls throughout your garden enjoying every step of the way! 🪶

field of poppies
(Fran Wershler)

Uninvited Annuals
by Frances Wershler

Fran is a longtime Prairie Garden Committee member and former Editor. She gardens in the St James area of Winnipeg, MB

Even in our gardens we have volunteers showing up faithfully whether we requisition them or not. I'm talking of those plants that self-seed around the place they are planted. Most plants that do this are annuals but some are biennial and a few are perennial.

Just how welcome these spontaneous assistants become, really depends on you and your type of garden. If you are the kind of person who has always yearned for a little English cottage garden, you will be delighted to have them. If, on the other hand, you are a plant collector with numerous specimen plants arranged so each can be shown off and admired for its own special beauty, you may not like a host of daisies, Johnny-jump-ups, poppies, forget-me-nots or dame's rocket that just seize a nice patch of soil among the other plants and grow on to maturity.

In his book **Crazy About Gardening**, Canadian author Des Kennedy says, "It's a sobering realization that a fair bit of what passes for clever planning at our place is more the result of the lunch bucket work of dependable volunteers and happy accidents. In spring more than a few of our self-celebrated plantings are rescued from dull contrivance and made brilliant by the spreading foam of clear blue forget-me-nots, their countless tiny yellow-eyed flowers brushing the garden with a hazy, lovely wash of blue."

My own garden finds itself swathed in forget-me-nots in spring, only to be cleansed of their presence as I snatch armfuls of the plants when they begin to reseed. They will return unless weeded out. Tiny plant replacements soon begin to appear to succeed the lost ones so some further weeding is necessary at regular times. I like to see the odd dame's rocket pop up among the gas plants and some Shirley poppies are not an unpleasant addition on the edge of a bed. I've traded blue columbine seed heads that were likely first seeded by the birds for larkspur seeds a friend picked out of her front flower bed where they grew at random.

Some of these unbidden guests are particularly suited to our Prairie gardens. When purchasing flower seed, look for the term 'hardy annual' and know that these flowers may be easy to grow and will be long lasting plants. Many of these varieties hang around even after the first killing frost and they'll keep on blooming and setting seed as well. A good time to plant these varieties is autumn, when they naturally set seed. Many of us deadhead the early blooming plants because of this habit since they can seed too generously. Some gardeners leave a few seed pods or one mother plant to drop seeds. If there is a place in the garden where they would be appropriate, we just shake a seed head or pod in that area.

It is important to remember that if we wish seeds from our garden plants to grow next spring they usually need the cold temperatures of winter to make the seeds viable. If they don't self seed and you do not spread seed in the autumn, place them in the freezer for a few weeks before spring planting.

A special note in favour of self seeding plants is that they are among the plants that will grow quickly and spark an interest from the children who visit your garden. The seeds are usually easy to plant and grow quickly enough that small gardeners are intrigued to

watch their progress with the result that they become interested in the garden. When plants they sowed last year reappear the following year, those youngsters may be even more excited about their contribution to the garden. There are few things more satisfying for young and old than raising plants from seed to flower.

Some Famous Volunteer Plants

Johnny Jump-Up (*Viola cornuta*) are violas with an old-fashioned looking, small, pansy-like blossom which appears in spring and blooms quite unobtrusively among other plants. They have edible flowers that will make a great garnish on a salad.

Love-in-a-mist (*Nigella damascena*) is a wonderful, clear blue, pink or white annual flower. We can appreciate it for its architectural look when the seed pods come after the flowers. If you pick some pods when they have burgundy stripes, you can dry them for winter flower arrangements.

Love-in-a-mist (*Nigella damascena*) (Wildfleur)

Calendula (*Calendula officinalis*) or Pot Marigolds that are left to their own devices can lighten up garden beds for many years with bright orange and yellow flowers. When all the other annual flowers have been ravaged by early frost, this annual is still going strong.

Cleome, Spider Flower (*Cleome hassleriana*) is one of the best self-seeders. It can be a three foot tall plant and it has large pink, white, rose or purple flower heads arranged in a loose ball shape. I first admired cleome growing out between patio stones at a Prairie Garden Committee member's home. Gardeners should be selective about where they allow this visitor to grow because of the height it may attain..

Feverfew (*Tanacetum parthenium*) sometimes acts as a biennial, but in climate zones lower than five, such as we have on the Prairies, it usually self-seeds. Small single daisy-like flowers or double white button shaped flowers appear on low bush-like plants with citrus scented leaves. It has been grown as a medicinal plant for many years.

Bachelor buttons, Cornflower (*Centaurea cyanus*) is one of our few blue garden flowers. It can cause friction if planted in community gardens because it is notorious for self seeding indiscriminately. If you garden in a community area it is not a good idea to plant these old fashioned plants as borders around your garden plot.

Annual Baby's Breath (*Gyposophila elegans*) is a dainty low growing white flower that makes a wonderful addition to flower arrangements and looks attractive in a flowerbed. It is not a prolific multiplier but grows quickly, blooms heavily and dies with the first frost. It rarely becomes a nuisance in a garden.

Dame's rocket, Sweet rocket (*Hesperis matronalis*) is a common garden plant in the mustard family introduced from Eurasia and hardy to zone 3. It can be very invasive, but many gardeners find it attractive and let it grow where they need some tall plants for background interest. The sweet-scented flowers range from white to several shades of pink and purple and grow in terminal racemes (each flower has its own little stalk branching off the main stem). Long, narrow seed pods follow the flowers and should be removed as soon as possible to prevent the plant from becoming a nuisance.

Some other plants that will re-seed are: Alyssum, Shirley poppies, French marigolds, gomphrena, larkspur, snapdragon, nasturtium and nicotiana. 🦗

See page 91 for photos.

Gardening requires lots of water, most of it in the form of perspiration.

Impatiens
Busy Lizzy has never been busier
by Dorothy Dobbie

Dorothy Dobbie is the owner and publisher of the Local Gardener magazines, Manitoba Gardener, Ontario Gardener and Alberta Gardener. She also broadcasts a weekly gardening show on CJOB in Winnipeg.

In some parts of England, "busy Lizzie" (*Impatiens walleriana*) is considered a very lowly flower, grown by those who can't grow anything else. But today's gardener knows there's more to the humble impatiens than used to meet the eye.

First of all, it's not just a shade plant – although it rewards in shade. Given enough water, impatiens will thrive in heat and bright sunshine. It is one of the stock-in-trade flowers used at Disneyland, where its glowing colours make it ideal for planting in a medium to float in ponds.

I. walleriana comes from the tropics, eastern Africa to be exact, but it's a forgiving plant, happy to adapt to short summers in cold climates such as ours.

In some quarters, it is called touch-me-not, for its exploding seed pods, which will disperse their bounty with great emphasis. Not only that, but impatiens have the ability to change sex. The flowers are male when they first open, then shed their pollen cap revealing their female organs. This is a strategy to keep them from self-pollinating. Symbolic of motherly love, they were called Our Lady's earrings in medieval times.

Impatiens are prolific and reliable bloomers, needing no deadheading. They like a soil rich in organic materials, especially compost or well-rotted manure. Pinching back will encourage branching, producing a fuller, rounder-shaped plant.

It's easy to propagate impatiens through cuttings, which can be taken in spring or fall and set to root with a little rooting compound. They can also be rooted in water or in moistened sand or soil.

Double impatiens are truly rewarding, with rose-like flowers of about one-inch in diameter. They are upright plants, growing 23–30 cm (9–12 in) and put on a fabulous show for the entire summer.

Impatiens walleriana has lots of cousins; there are over 1,000 species in the impatiens family, not the least of which is the well-favoured New Guinea impatiens. With a stronger stem and more prominent, heavily veined leaf that comes in green, bronze, maroon and variegated cream-on-green, New Guineas generally have larger flowers that are 5–6½ cm

(2-2½ in) in diameter—in stunning shades such as fuchsia, lavender and orange. They appeared on the scene in North America in 1970, after being found in their namesake country.

New Guineas love water; their natural habitat is on the margins of streams. Half a day's sun with filtered sun in the hottest part of the day will keep these beauties blooming at their best. Flowering stops when temperatures exceed 29° C (84° F).

Latest on the scene is the fabled yellow impatiens, several hybrid varieties of which have recently appeared on the market. Developed from a variety of different wild stock, including the North American Yellow Jewelweed (*Impatiens pallida*) [see page 29], unfavourable characteristics have been bred out of these new varieties so that they behave in the garden.

Burpee sells a lovely slipper-shaped impatiens they call 'African Blondie', which has yellow stripes at its heart and Ball has developed one called 'Fusion

Yellow' which has more open petal formation with a rosy glow in the centre.

There is also an *Impatiens balsamina*, Rose balsam, available commercially. This plant grows up to 75 cm (2½ ft) tall and has serrated, pointed leaves and orchid-like flowers in pink to mauve hues. *I. balsamina* is native to south eastern Asia. Juice from its stems and leaves are used to treat warts and snakebite and the flower is applied to burns to cool the skin.

Impatiens grow all over the world, right up to the arctic. Some are considered weeds and gardeners either love them or hate them, but nobody can ignore them. From dear little busy Lizzie to the fantastic doubles and flashy yellows or the weedy *I. pallida* or *I. repens* (a creeping variety from Sri Lanka), impatiens make their presence known though their explosive seeds and their brilliant colours.

No matter what your taste, there's an impatiens for you.   ❧
See page 91 for photos.

Falling for Flowers (the Cool Ones!)
by Carla Hrycyna

"The feel of earth, the fresh scent of soil and the unmistakable fragrance of a flower inspires gardeners, new and experienced, with the passion to nurture their own piece of earth." C. Hrycyna

Spring is an inspirational time of year, with preparations underway for planning and planting the garden. We busy ourselves searching through seed catalogues and magazines that entice us with mature landscape views, gardens bursting with colour and patios beautifully decked out in colourfully designed containers—all to feed the personal need of 'the gardener' to begin the next season. I truly believe spring is the beginning of a cycle: summer the transition, and fall the completion. For many, fall is the 'grand finale', revered in its ultimate glory, growth, colour palette and structural display.

The fall garden is at its best with colourful displays of fall flowering and foliage plants (sunflowers, rudbeckias, pansies, garden mums, Swiss chard, flowering cabbage (or kale). All of these in their glory, have extended blooming power and vigour with the change in temperature, from intense summer temperatures to the cool crisper air of fall.

Combinations of heights, ranging from 15 cm (6 in) to over 2 m (6 ft), occur in various plants during the fall. Their rich tones of red, golden yellow, orange, rust and purple contribute to the warmth of the garden. It is with the new fall season that the gardener has renewed energy to be back in the garden.

Sunflowers
(*Helianthus annuus*)

Sunflowers belonging to the Asteraceae family are divided into three classes. Dwarf $^{1}/_{3}$–$^{3}/_{4}$ m (1–2$^{1}/_{2}$ ft), intermediate 1–1$^{1}/_{2}$ m (3–5 ft), and tall 1$^{1}/_{2}$–2$^{1}/_{2}$ m (5–8 ft). Sunflowers are so representative of the prairies. When you drive through the countryside from early August through to fall, one is often enthralled with sunflower fields. City residents can mimic that look by planting selections of sunflowers to accent their own fall display. Planted as soldiers, tall sunflowers give height to the garden, while shorter varieties are perfect for the front of the border, or for use in container gardening. Attracting bees and butterflies to the garden during the early stages of their growth, sunflowers are also a food source to birds as the centre discs of the flower reach maturity. Pollenless sunflowers are perfect for those gardeners with allergies and they have a tendency to last longer as a cut flower. Both pollen and pollen-less sunflowers produce seeds.

Dwarf Sunflowers:
- 'Big Smile' – is 30–38 cm (12–15 in) tall with a 15 cm (6 in) disc head with black centres.
- 'Teddy Bear' – a double (pom-pom-like), 8–13 cm (3–5 in) bloom on well branched stems. Grows to 38 cm (15 in) tall.
- 'Firecracker' - grows to $^{3}/_{4}$ m (2.5 ft) tall with a central black disc with red petals radiating to yellow tips on the petals.

Intermediate Sunflowers:
- 'Ring of Fire' - 1–1$^{1}/_{2}$ m (3–5 ft) tall bicolour flower similar to 'Firecracker' in petal colour with multi-branched stems.
- 'Sunbright Supreme' - grows 1$^{1}/_{4}$–1$^{1}/_{2}$ m (4–5 ft) tall with pollen-less, bright yellow flowers with a dark brown centre.

Tall Sunflowers:
- 'Sunbright'- reaching almost 2 m (7 ft) tall with a single soft yellow bloom.
- 'Ruby'- bright red blooms on 1½ m (5 ft) tall, pollen-less. The leaves of this variety have a reddish tone on the stem. Unique!

Rudbeckia
Rudbeckias are rich in colour, similar to sunflowers with tones ranging in yellow, to rust, to red. Either single 'daisy-like' or pompom style, blooms are held on plants ranging from 25–91 cm (10– 36 in) tall. Daisy style rudbeckias have either green or black centres. The blooms range in size from 7½ cm (3 in) wide (i.e. *Rudbeckia* 'Corona' to almost 20 cm (8 in) wide (i.e. *Rudbeckia* 'Denver Daisy')
- 'Becky' – grows 30 cm (12 in) tall with multi-stems of various colour types ranging from cinnamon bicolour, to yellow.
- 'Cherry Brandy' - growing 60 cm (24 in) tall. This newer variety has 7½ cm (3 in) daisy-like blooms in deep wine red.
- 'Cherokee Sunset' – pom-pom double blooms in shades of yellow, rust and red are held high at 76 cm (30 in) tall blooming freely from July well into frost.

Flowering Cabbage/Kale
(*Brassica oleracea*)
Flowering Cabbage/Kale are fall flowering foliage plants gaining popularity in the landscape. In either a smooth leaf, wavy leaf or feathered forms, these 'cabbage-like' plants of white, to pink, to purple, to red stand out sharply in the garden during cooler fall temperatures when warm season annuals are stressed. The leaves of *Brassica oleracea* have a waxy or rubbery feel to them. Unlike other flowering annuals, flowering cabbage has no 'flower' per se, instead, the central growth of the cabbage is the 'floral accent' of the plant. The central parts of the cabbage are generally brighter in colour than the outer leaves. Varieties are available for cut flowers as with *Brassica oleracea* 'Crane' series, with 15 cm (6 in) long stemmed in pink, red and rose.
- Round-leaf (Flowering Cabbage) spread to almost 46 cm (18 in) wide, and 15–30 cm (6–12 in) tall. Seek selections such as Dynasty (Osaka) Series or Pigeon Series.
- Wavy-leaf types (Flowering Kale) spread 30–71 cm (12–28 in) wide and 30–61 cm (12–24 in) tall. Look for Emperor (Nagoya Series) or Chidori Red. If desiring an edible type of Kale try Lacinato Kale 'Dinosaur' (blue green leaves).
- Flowering Cabbage/Kale are cool season plants. They perform best when grown in full sun. As the plant grows larger, the central portion intensifies in colour (especially when the late fall temperatures turn cooler). Like all others in the 'cabbage' family, regular dusting

of the plants with an insecticide is beneficial for its growth.

Chrysanthemum

Chrysanthemums are also known as the Garden Mum or Fall Mum. These have my vote for being the 'work-horses' of the fall garden. Their dense growth, with masses of flower heads, create a huge impact in the garden in a full colour range of yellows, purples, reds, rusts and white. The fall mum comes in the forms of daisy (singles), pom-pom (ball shaped), or semi-double (decorative) or button (smaller than 2½ cm/1 in). Care should be given when weeding or working near mums as the foliage is brittle and easy to break. Give mums plenty of room. In my experience, mums are not totally hardy. As with any other perennial, weather is factor with this plant surviving a winter. The Prairies bring a challenge to any gardener, making garden mums an experiment in achieving success. An exemplary show of garden mums outweigh the work of adding extra mulch to the base of the plants to aid in their survival.

Swiss Chard

Swiss chard is a vegetable, often treated as an ornamental annual. Related to beets, Swiss chard has stalks that look similar to rhubarb, and leaves that look like spinach. Both the stems and leaves are edible (though not as tasty as spinach). Look for Swiss Chard 'Bright Lights' with striking stem colours of fuchsia, red, yellow, orange, pink and gold topped with bright green to bronze coloured leaves.

Pansies

Probably the most famous of the cool season flowers are pansies. Pansies are predominantly used in the spring and are rejuvenated in the fall. Pansies/violas, whether small or large faced (from 2½–8 cm/1–3 in), bob their heads gently in the breeze on top of 10–25 cm (4–10 in) tall plants. It is the colourful face of the pansy, so reminiscent of those seen in our storybooks of *Alice in Wonderland*, that bring smiles to the faces of those who adorn their gardens with these plants. Whether choosing solid coloured varieties (Matrix Series), heavily ruffled petals (Frizzle Sizzle Series), or pansies with whiskers (Whiskers Series), there are literally hundreds of pansies in a full colour pallet.

In combination with late season perennials, the fall garden, co-ordinated with these cool-loving annuals will be a hit.

Recommended late season perennials would include: Ornamental grasses (i.e. *Calamagrostis* 'Karl Foerster'), *Sedum* ('Autumn Joy'), *Solidago*, Aster ('Purple Dome') and *Heliopsis* 'Summer Sun'. 🦋

See page 92 for photos.

Marigolds

by Miles Duncan – Landscape Technician

Miles has been employed with St. Mary's Nursery and Garden Centre for 25 years. He possesses a vast knowledge and experience with trees, shrubs, annuals and perennials.

Marigolds have been around for hundreds of years and have not only been used for colour in the garden but also for medical purposes. Marigold (*Tagetes*) is sometimes called Goldes, Ruddes, Mary Gowles, Oculus Christi, Marygold and Fiore D'agnimese.

Here on the prairies, there are only a few Marigold varieties we are familiar with, such as the African Marigold (*Tagetes erecta*) which grows in a mounding, compact form about 30-40 cm (12-16 in) high. The double flowers are at least 8 cm (3 in) in diameter and cover the whole plant. The colour ranges from gold to soft yellow to orange. One of the varieties includes the Crush series. The French Marigold (*Tagetes patula*) is a dwarf compact plant that ranges in height from 20-25 cm (8-10 in) with blooms that are 5 cm (2 in) in size. Some of the varieties in this series include Bonanza, Little Hero, and Safari. The colours range from bright yellow to red and orange and even bi-colours. The Signet Marigold (*Tagetes tenuifolia*) has a fine leaf structure and very small single flowers and is planted in rock gardens for splashes of colour. They are about 10 cm (4 in) in height and a familiar variety is the Gem series.

Some varieties for warmer climates include:
• Tangerine scented Marigold (*Tagetes lemonii*) that have a lemon/mint scent and grow to about 1 m (3 ft) in height.
• Spanish Tarragon Marigold (*Tagetes lucida*) produces small anise flavoured flowers.
• Irish Lace Marigold (*Tagetes filifolia*) is a short plant, having lacy leaves and small white flowers.
• Pot Marigold (*Calendula officinalis*) is not a true Marigold (but looks very much like a Marigold) and has bright yellow to orange flowers.

Marigold
(Matti Paavonen)

Marigolds are considered very easy to grow and are great for mass plantings and containers. The colours range from yellows and reds to white offering wide colour choice in the garden. They like well-drained soil and will bloom right into fall. Good deep watering is a must at the start followed by a regimen of regular watering.

Plant spacing should be about 20-40 cm (8-16 in) apart and in full sun, deadheading is a must to force continual blooming. They should only be planted outside after the last frost because they cannot tolerate any freezing weather.

A common myth surrounding Marigolds is that if you plant them with your vegetables, they will keep insect pests out of your garden. However, research has shown that it appears to make no difference to the damage caused to the vegetable crops. Spider mites seem to be one of the few insects that attack them directly.

Historic medicinal use of the Marigold was for treating headaches, jaundice, red eyes, sore eyes and toothaches. A potion was once made up for under-water divers to help slow down their heart rate for deeper dives. The flower itself rubbed directly onto a bee sting or wasp bite is supposed to relieve the pain. Lotion made from the flowers is said to be useful for sprains and wounds. It's even believed to help lower fevers.

Macer's Herbal states that Marigolds will bring out evil humours and help the eyes.

Golde is bitter in savour
Fayr and zelw is his flowur
Ye golde flour is good to sene
It makyth ye syth bryth and clene
Wyscely to lokyn on his flowres
Drawyth owt of ye heed wikked hirores

This is a natural insecticide/fungicide formula that you may want to give a try:

1. Add large amounts of Marigold flowers, leaves and roots to a bucket of water.

2. Let stand 5-7 days, stirring once a day.

3. Once decayed, strain mixture though a cloth, keeping the liquid only.

4. Dilute with soapy water (Potash based soaps only).

5. Spray crops before problems start and continue weekly applications.

This natural insecticide/fungicide is said to strengthen potatoes, beans, tomatoes, and peas to help resist blight, mildew, and other fungal diseases. It can also be used to repel aphids, flies, caterpillars, moths, ants, maggots, termites, and nematodes.

Marigolds are a staple in prairie gardens, adding colourful interest and they are steeped in lore as to their usefulness. 🐦

See page 93 for photos.

Touch-Me-Not
by Shirley Froehlich

Shirley is the owner of Prairie Originals, a nursery specialising in wildflowers, prairie grasses, native shrubs and vines for landscaping.

The first time I saw this plant I was in Sandilands forest in southeast Manitoba. I noticed it for two reasons: it was 5 feet tall (150cm) and there were hummingbirds visiting the flowers. I had to find out what it was. I later discovered that it was Touch-Me-Not (*Impatiens capensis*). Other common names for it are Jewelweed, Orange Balsam and Lady's Earrings. In the past the latin name was *Impatiens biflora*.

Description

Touch-Me-Not is one of our few native annuals. It is generally a well branched, bushy plant growing from 60-150 cm (2-5 ft) tall. The leaves are alternate and oval varying from 2.5-10 cm (1-4 in) long. The thick, juicy stems are often tinged with red. The showy, irregular flowers are orange with many reddish brown spots. The flowers have a long, curving nectar filled spur at the back. Hummingbirds come for the nectar and pollinate the flowers at the same time. The bill of the bird picks up the grains of white pollen from just inside the top front of one flower and deposits them on the inside top of the next. It blooms from July to September. The pod-like seed capsules spring open as the seed ripens to eject the seed up to four or five feet. The capsules are sensitive to touch even before the seed is ripe. This is probably how the plant got its name. Touch-Me-Not can produce seed even without being pollinated by hummingbirds because they have cleistogamous flowers just like violets. Cleistogamous flowers often appear later in the season. They never open but they contain all the necessary parts to produce fertile seeds. The sensitive, exploding pods make collecting seed a challenge for this plant. I find it easiest to set a tray under the plants in summer and let the plants seed the tray themselves.

This beautiful, lush looking plant is quite succulent and juicy when crushed. The juice from the plant was historically used to treat poison ivy and nettle stings. However, the effectiveness of this treatment has been discounted in recent years after several clinical trials.

Native Habitat

This plant has a wide native range, growing all across Canada and throughout most of the United States except the southwest. It grows in a wide range of soils from sandy to heavy clay with the critical factor being good moisture. Touch-Me-Not doesn't grow in dry locations. In the wild it can be found in moist areas along lake-shores, rivers, creeks and ditches as well as in moist to wet woodlands, generally in part to full shade.

Culture

Touch-Me-Not grows in sun or shade as long as it has very good moisture. Since it is an annual, it grows very fast and it relies on reseeding to continue from year to year. It seeds prolifically and becomes a thick carpet in moist growing conditions. To get a patch established you probably only need to start with a few plants. If you find your patch becomes a little larger than you want, it is very easy to control. The roots are very shallow making it easy to pull out or knock over.

If you want to start it from seed indoors, the seed should be stratified (a cold, moist treatment) for 6 weeks and then germinated at 21 degrees. I generally find it easiest to let it self seed and germinate outdoors and then dig and transplant small seedlings to other locations or to pots. Give some extra shade for a few weeks after transplanting and transplant when it is not too hot.

Touch-Me-Not is suitable for natural settings such as at the cottage, in woodland gardens or along streams, ditches and other wet areas. Wherever you plant it, you will find hummingbirds coming to visit the beautiful, nectar filled jewels hanging like Lady's Earrings on the plant. 🦋

The puzzle about where to plant spring bulbs

You want to see them when they first bloom and you do not want to see the dying foliage. Plan where they will go by looking out your kitchen window or your front door so you can put them right where you can see them. Plant them in the centre of the flowerbed so that growing perennials will block the view of leaves dying back after flowering has finished.

Petunias
by John Van Beveren

John Van Beveren has been a sales representative for Ball Horticultural Company for 30 years. He has a Diploma in Horticulture from the University of Guelph. John and his wife enjoyed gardening in Manitoba for 32 years. They now live in British Columbia.

Back when I started as a salesman, there were only two types of petunias: multiflora and grandiflora. Multifloras were small flowered varieties and grandifloras were large bloomed varieties. I was then considered a petunia expert, pretty simple. Today the industry has bred a large product offering that will satisfy any and every gardening need. I know the question you are asking yourself—WHY? Well, petunias look great in the garden and survive a wide range of environmental conditions, which makes it easier to grow a showy garden that lasts all summer.

Thanks to these breeding efforts, we now have:

- **milliflora** - compact, miniature plants that produce huge quantities of small flowers only 2-2.5 cm (1-1.5 in) in diameter.
- **multiflora** - huge number of blossoms
- **floribunda** - spreading growth pattern
- **grandiflora** - large flowers
- **trailing** (flat and upright) long flower covered stems
- **trailing milliflora**, **trailing multiflora** and **trailing grandiflora.**

Petunia hanging basket (Valerie Denesiuk)

The goods news is there is plenty of selection. The bad news is, of course, choosing what to plant and deciding where in your garden it should go. With all of this variety and selection, being an expert in petunias has changed. The best way to select interesting varieties for your yard is to visit and speak with my customers—your local garden centre professionals.

Planting petunias in your yard is easy. They grow well in highlight, low-light, in the ground, and in containers, which is currently one of the most popular ways petunias are grown. Petunias, however, are hungry devils, and it is important to feed them regularly, or at least put in a slow release fertilizer that emits a bit of food each time you water.

Now the fun part – my favourite varieties. Number one on the list is Purple Wave. This is the titan of petunias. The only thing that can stop it is Kryptonite (and a pot with no drainage holes). A whole family of Waves have been created with different flower sizes, colours, and habits (plant shapes). These include the original Waves, Easy Waves, Tidal Waves, Double Waves, and the latest addition, Shock Waves.

My second favourite is Madness Petunias, which were the first floribunda petunias on the market. They are a cross between a grandiflora and a multiflora. Madness have the garden performance of a multiflora, but with a larger flower. They are very uniform in height and easy to maintain, requir-ing less dead-heading (picking off the dead flowers). Madness are very popular with parks because of their low maintenance and selection of over twenty colours. Madness also have a series of double bloomed petunias called Double Madness.

My third favourite is a tough little guy called the Picobella series (formerly known as Fantasy petunias). This is a smaller plant and flower than Madness or Waves; they are an excellent choice for mixed containers as they stay compact, with tons of small flowers. They also do not dominate other less vigorous plants in the container (they play well with others).

My fourth favourite are Potunias. This is a new series of petunias that are best suited to be grown in a hanging basket. The plant grows in a round ball shape and when mature will look like a flower bubble. These are very low maintenance plants, requiring little or no dead-heading. A good colour selection is making this an increasingly popular choice for hanging baskets.

I hope this sheds some light on the world of petunias. They are always an excellent choice for the Prairies. My garden in Manitoba always had them, and even though I experimented with different unique items, you can't beat the show and reliability that the petunia gives your garden. 🐾

See page 96 for photos.

Understanding Coleus: the Garden's Kaleidoscope

by Dr. Bob Bors

Bob Bors is the Project Leader of the Domestic Fruit Program and an Assistant Professor in the Department of Plant Sciences with the University of Saskatchewan. Bob's research focuses on breeding, tissue culture, propagation, disease screening, and interspecific hybridization of horticultural crops with emphasis on fruit and ornamentals.

During my 1st year as a professor at the University of Saskatchewan I received a rather vicious letter from a nursery company stating that I would be prosecuted if I was illegally propagating any of their varieties. I was in shock. How would I ever get tenure if some nursery was taking me to court? Could it be that one of my students had ratted on me for propagating coleus? I hadn't considered that some of the coleus might be registered under Plant Breeder's Rights (PBR). Most of the coleus in the University collection didn't have name tags.

I decided then and there to move the coleus collection to the greenhouse that had bees, let them get cross pollinated, go to seed and create my own coleus. Years later I found that horrible letter and realized it was a computer generated form letter from a rose company. They had sent it to all members of the Canadian Ornamental Plant Foundation (COPF) (www.copf.

org). By then I was already three generations into my coleus breeding addiction and using the plants in four classes. Now I'm into my ninth year of breeding them! Those of you who know me for fruit breeding, don't worry. Working with coleus is a part time activity for me, mostly done in the coldest parts of winter.

So, is it illegal to propagate coleus that have plant breeder's rights? Yes it is, but it is highly unlikely that any company would prosecute gardeners or teachers; nurseries maybe. For me, a knowingly illegally propagated plant loses it beauty and would be a constant reminder of being too cheap to buy the extra plants desired. Most coleus don't have plant breeder's rights. Some coleus are trademarked, which means you can't use the name without permission, but it's perfectly legal to propagate it. When you buy a coleus plant at a nursery, the label will usually mention 'PBR' (Canada), plant patents (USA), trademarks, or 'COPF registered' if such rights exist.

The latter is an honour system among nurseries which is an ingenious way to inspire plant breeders with royalties, without the huge expense and time delay of going through Plant Breeders Rights.

Why are some coleus so different?

Over the next few years you will likely see more interesting coleus varieties being introduced by nurseries. A key reason for the huge amount of variation in coleus is that there were originally around 17 species that were bred into many of the new varieties. This has led to a wide range of colours and leaf shapes.

Colour

Colour change in coleus is due to several reasons. Higher plants (those with vascular tissues) have cell layers (called histogenic layers) that usually give rise to similarly coloured cells, but in coleus, each cell layer can be a different colour. This can result in a patterned leaf that has different colours in the centre and outer portions of the leaves. A great example of this is the variety 'Saturn'. For some varieties the underside and top part of the leaves of coleus are different. In addition to pigment production, coleus can have layers with no chlorophyll, (white) or low levels (light green) or high levels (dark green). Because coleus leaves are rather thin, light passes through the layers and can blend the colours. If, for instance, you have a leaf that makes only red pigments but has the 3 layers of different chlorophyll, you can get pink, bright red and dark red.

If you are getting dizzy, sit down, I'm not done yet. The production of red and purple pigments by coleus is highly affected by temperatures. Warm or hot temperatures can increase red and purple, while cold snaps decrease them. The colour production of any given leaf, however, becomes fixed during the time when the leaf is young and still growing, and becomes more stable once the leaf is mature. So the younger leaves of a plant can be one shade and older leaves another shade. This is further complicated by the decline of chlorophyll in older leaves, which can make red turn into pink.

When grown from seed, plants may be solidly green or purple when having only a few leaves but may dramatically change as they get to their 3rd or 4th set of leaves. Reds, yellows and orange colours often begin to develop once the plant makes larger leaves.

Stripes, spots and dust

Some coleus have genes that cause instability between the histogenic cell layers. This causes cell layers to flip, so that the colour on the bottom is now on the top and vice versa, thus creating variegation. Sometimes that gene causes large sections of leaves to change in irregular stripes and occasionally may give rise to a shoot that is only one colour. I call it the 'drop cloth effect' when only small flecks of different colour result. The flecks can be so small that it looks like some dust has fallen onto your plants. Variegation can also be caused by colour genes being turned on or off – no flipping required!

To Shade or Not to Shade

Coleus are adapted to lower light levels. Indoors, I always put mine in a sunny window (glass removes most of the UV light). Outside, I prefer to put them in areas of semi-shade, neither completely in the shade nor only in the sun. In more recent years varieties have been released as 'sun-tolerant'. Just as in humans, darker pigments help protect them tagainst damaging UV light. The new sun-tolerant types often have dark or bright pigments but likely won't have white, yellow or pink in them. I really like the colour of the sun-tolerant 'Texas Parking Lot' which is a nice stable orange red (orange in other varieties tends to fade or burn especially in the sun). Even sun-tolerant varieties do best in semi-shade. However, if you want coleus in yellow, light green, or if it has splashes of white, it's best to put them in shadier locations. Lighter coloured leaves get sunburned which leads to brown portions on the leaves, especially when a long cloudy period is followed by very sunny hot days.

Leaf Shape

When first introduced in the Victorian era, coleus had rather simple large heart shaped leaves. For a hundred years, coleus all had similar shaped leaves. However, the last two decades, have seen 'breakthrough' varieties introducing new leaf shapes. Thomson and Morgans' 'Dragon Sunset and Volcano mixed' has wavy leaves in a wide range of colours. 'Kiwi Fern' takes waviness to a new extreme with leaves that look like fine combs. 'Inky fingers' has more of a paw print look. Many new varieties have ruffled edges. 'Tilt-a-Whirl' is another unusual, rather fun shaped leaf that swirls.

In my own breeding program I developed some plants I call 'lobsters' which have sections of leaves

This amazing coleus plant below was 'born' with exactly one side with a colour gene on and the other side with the gene off. Eventually, it only had shoots that were burgundy or green. I used to call it Yin/Yang.

held on by veins. I've also developed some that have extremely complex leaves that have multiple layers. 'Buttons' are another type developed at the U of SK which may be entering trials this summer in the US. I haven't seen any like these on the market yet but it's probably only a matter of time.

Blooming

While some gardeners like coleus blooms, they are not considered desirable. Flowers are either purple or white which can be an undesirable contrast with the coloured leaves. Even those who like the flowers will find them ugly when they turn brown. Heavy seed production can sap the energy from the plant causing leaves to fade. They then give up trying to form new leaves.

Breeders have developed varieties that rarely bloom. I had 'Wedding Train' for several years and it never bloomed for me. Some varieties such as 'Pineapple' will bloom only under short days. Planting varieties such as these means you don't have to pinch them to keep them looking nice in summer, but if you have them inside in winter they will start blooming. When you buy coleus seeds and plant them (or if your nursery grows them from seeds) these types love to flower all summer long. This is the fault I find with the 'Kong' series which otherwise is impressive for having huge leaves on short stocky plants.

All of the nicer cultivars are vegetatively propagated. They are unlikely to come true from seed. Saving seeds from one of the highly changing varieties such as 'Shizophrenia' can result in a whole family of different coloured offspring.

Plant structure

Older coleus varieties, such as 'Wizard Mix' have rather thick stems that are prone to break especially if allowed to grow tall and if placed in a windy spot. Breaking can be greatly reduced by periodic pinching to develop a multi-branched plant. However, these older types can be trained as a 'standard' (a topiary shape) to be one of the most spectacular coleus of all (*See box next page*). The general trend for newer varieties, though, is for plants with wispy shoots that don't grow very tall, and are unlikely to break, thus needing less care.

Coleus Companies

In an attempt to get my own coleus into the market place, I discovered Canadian nurseries prefer to import coleus cuttings rather than keep their own stock plants. Coleus can easily become infested with mealy bugs and many Canadian greenhouses like to shut down during mid winter to save energy, so where would they keep coleus stock plants? Instead, they order from international companies who grow their coleus outside in Central America, Mexico, or the Caribbean during the winter. Fields of coleus are

Training a Coleus Standard

- Don't choose a dwarf variety. Older varieties grown from seeds will often get taller than clonally propagated varieties.
- I prefer to use ceramic or clay pots as they are heavier and less likely to fall over.
- Allow the plant to grow straight up and only pinch the tip when a flower appears or when the plant gets to the desired height.
- Remove all side shoots on the bottom 2/3rds of the plant. But let the top 1/3rd form new shoots.

- When the top few buds break, let them grow a few leaves then pinch the tip. This will cause the top to become bushy.
- Continue to pinch on a regular basis. If any branches break off, consider that a message to be more drastic on pruning.
- Stake your plant if you think there is danger of it breaking.
- Coleus standards can last a few years if you have good conditions even in winter. Stems can get quite wide and tough, but you must always be mindful about pruning them.

harvested for cuttings and shipped to nurseries across Canada just when they need them in early spring. While varieties can change from year to year, you will find the same new varieties appearing simultaneously across the country. Within the last year companies from Japan, California and Florida have visited the U of SK and have been evaluating our coleus. Ideally, the coleus will be grown at a Caribbean nursery which I will need to visit each winter for consultations!

University of Saskatchewan Varieties

In 2008, we released four varieties at Saskatoon's Gardenscape show. They were named for different times of the day: Sunrise, Sunnyday, Sundown, and Night Time. Then in 2009, as a fund-raiser for Saskatoon's Persephone Theatre, the variety 'Audrey III' was released. This coleus looks particularly dangerous with sharply pointed 'teeth' and purple red veins. It will have been sold during the showing of the play "Little Shop of Horrors", which is about a man-eating plant named 'Audrey II'.

Ultimate Coleus Website

For more information, absolutely the best coleus website in the world is www.coleusfinder.org. This website gathers coleus pics and links and has an impressive database that can be searched by colour and leaf shape. At last count over 1400 varieties were listed! They even have a special article on the U of SK coleus breeding program at: http://www.coleusfinder.org/saskatchewan.php. On this web page you can download a large file with dozens of my coleus pictures. 🦋

See page 94-95 for photos.

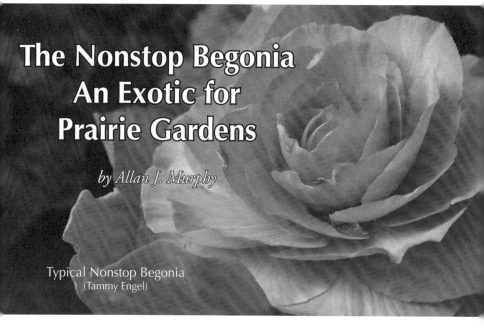

The Nonstop Begonia
An Exotic for
Prairie Gardens

by Allan J. Murphy

Typical Nonstop Begonia
(Tammy Engel)

Until the 1970's, it was unusual to find tuberous begonias being grown locally except in the gardens of the most serious enthusiast or in the occasional institutional planting. Availability of the tubers, cost, the difficulty of providing the right growing conditions indoors in early March, all of these and other concerns proved to be an undertaking all but the most enthusiastic gardeners were not prepared to make. All of this changed, however, when in 1972 the storied German seed company Benary, released what we know as the 'Nonstop Begonia', so called because under appropriate conditions these plants may be induced to flower year round. It is an F1 hybrid (see note below), which can be treated much the same as most annuals. Seed sown in early January will be ready for sale by the end of May. In order to appreciate the significance of this breeding achievement and its role in popularizing these magnificent flowering plants, it is necessary to trace briefly the history of the genus *Begonia* in Western horticulture.

The mid 19th century was the heyday of the professional plant explorer, something which from our perspective now seems unbelievably romantic. Some of the larger nurseries in England and elsewhere financed expeditions which set out to scour the 'New World' in search of the unique and unusual in deference to the demands of a newly affluent gardening public. In fact a Mr. Pearce travelling for the firm of James Veitch of London, sent home several begonia species in the 1860's, the characteristics of which may still be observed in today's cultivars.

Authorities today list as many as fifteen hundred species belonging to the genus which are found in the tropical and sub-tropical regions of the globe, but chiefly in the Americas. They became an instant sensation when they were made available to grace the conservatories and orangeries of the wealthy. Members of the genus hybridize quite freely and no sooner had they been introduced then gardeners began to take advantage of

this trait in attempts to develop new and ever more exotic forms.

Little is known about the parentage of these original crosses and the degree of secrecy usually associated with commercial hybridization makes a true botanical classification of present day forms all but impossible (but also unnecessary for our purposes).

One occasionally sees the term *Begonia* x *tuberhybrida*, in reference to hybrid tuberous begonias but it is far too general to be of much use. Some authors use the term 'standard', to refer to the older type, i.e. those grown from tubers and much taller than the newer Nonstops. This is the practice followed here. The term 'tuberous begonia' by itself refers to all members of the genus which produce tubers.

These original hybrids bore little resemblance to the large showy flowers we know today but it wasn't long before most of the work required to create fully double flowers was accomplished. While tuberous begonias are the main focus of this article, it seems necessary to mention some of the other well- known species since they still play an important role in horticulture. Probably the first of these to achieve widespread popularity was *B. semperflorens*, also known as 'Wax' or fibrous-rooted begonia. These became popular very early on and because of their waxy leaves and leaf colour that varies from bright green to a deep bronze, they were widely used in formal situations e.g. 'carpet bedding'. This group is enjoying a resurgence of popularity in the form of a recent cultivar 'Angel Wing', suitable for hanging baskets. Another group, once more popular than it is today, is made up of cultivars derived from the species *B. rex*. These plants are grown primarily for their interesting foliage, and typical of the group is one known as the 'Iron Cross' begonia. One other begonia of interest is *B. Hiemalis*, or 'Rieger' begonia, marketed here chiefly as a potted plant during the winter months.

But our concern here is the Nonstop and to understand just why its introduction was such an advance in begonia culture, the easiest way is to compare it with its predecessor, the tuberous type (standard), normally grown from mature tubers.

Plant Size: The original tuberous begonias could reach a height of twelve inches or more and invariably required staking. Nonstops are much shorter and if properly managed, should not require staking.

Flowers: The individual blossoms on the former could reach an enormous size, (one reads the description 'dinner plate' frequently, hopefully an exaggeration). A wide range of colours is available in both groups but a wide range of forms, referred to by descriptions such as Rosiflora Group, Camellia Group, Pendula Group and so on, is available only in the standard type. The arrangement of the flowers is the same, a large fully double female flower with two single, staminate flowers on either side.

Culture: Similar for established plants although propagation methods vary for each.

Period of Bloom: The older standards would normally produce one or two quite spectacular blossoms early in the season but then bloom only sporadically thereafter. But Nonstops, and this is where the major difference lies, are prolific bloomers, producing continuously until frost.

Pests, Diseases, etc.: Both types are remarkably trouble free although powdery mildew is a common problem which may be controlled by adequate sanitation procedures. Nonstops occasionally develop basal stem rot which normally results in the death of the plant. It remains to be seen what protective chemical measures may be available to gardeners in future.

Culture Of Nonstop Begonias
Since Nonstops have captured by far the largest part of market share, the remainder of this article will concentrate specifically on them. Newer varieties are being introduced continuously and I have by no means grown all of them. But I would suggest that most would respond favourably to these same conditions.

While it's unlikely that many of us will grow our plants from seed, this is how Nonstops are propagated and if one has the patience, it's not difficult.

The crop time from the date of sowing until flowering is about eighteen weeks. During that time the seedlings, which germinate in about ten days or so, require a strict regimen of light, temperature, and moisture. Not really different from any other seedling but the tolerances are much narrower. If one really wished to do it, it would be necessary to buy seed through an established nursery since seed is available only to the trade. Extremely tiny (50,000 seeds per gm.), it is pelleted and like other F1 hybrids, fairly expensive. Because of the time required, virtually all of the large growers that I am aware of locally, buy 'plugs', very small plants that are started by the thousands by speciality growers in warmer regions of the country and shipped here in time to be potted up and grown on by the retailer.

It is at this stage, some time in late May, that most of us will become involved, choosing to buy plants at our favourite nursery. What then to look for? Nonstops are normally grown on in four inch containers; anything smaller is inadequate. When making a purchase, look for plants that have good leaf colour. Avoid plants whose leaves appear slightly translucent or whitish in colour—a sign of poor culture. Plants should appear sturdy, stocky in appearance, being wider at the base than they are high. Plants that have had inadequate spacing in the greenhouse will tend to 'stretch'. Plants loaded with blossoms are quite naturally very seductive but it is better to be content with one or two of them and look instead for healthy buds making their way up from the base of the plant. Check to see that the base of the stem is fully developed and secure where it joins the roots. When taken out of the container, a secure mass of roots should be visible to the extremities of the soil mass.

Loose, aerated soils, rich in organic matter are preferred. Begonias are shallow rooted plants so soil depth is not that important but since they will be watered frequently, good drainage is essential. These plants cannot tolerate full sun and must be shielded from it at the hottest part of the day. Dappled sunlight provided by tree branches is ideal. Good air circulation will minimize fungal diseases mentioned earlier and keeping the area free of plant debris will reduce pest problems. Frequent light fertilizer applied several times during the growing season is necessary. Learn to assess the plants nutrient status based on leaf colour as a guide to fertilizer practice.

Despite their having been introduced almost four decades ago, one tends to think of Nonstops as 'new', since they are continually being discovered by an ever increasing gardening audience. Breeding efforts are continuing all the time, using conventional breeding techniques for the most part. While Nonstops do not as yet exhibit the variety of forms available in the older standards, these efforts have resulted in other advances, eg. single blossoms, varieties that are more tolerant of sun, and darker leaf colour (the Mocca Series). In the highly competitive world of seed production, introductions seem to be made at an increasing pace. Not all of these will find favour and some may only be available in markets other than ours. Those wishing to expand their knowledge of this remarkable genus will find the online site of the American Begonia Society very useful.

To end on a personal note, I should mention that I first saw the sensuous blooms of tuberous begonias in 1949 on a visit to a local park with my father. The attendant was a friend of his and tucked away in a corner, he nurtured his own little collection of begonias of which he was very proud. The following spring, I sent away to Dominion Seed House in Ontario to order some for myself. They came along beautifully until about mid-June, when, I suppose, I just couldn't accept the fact that exposing them to full sun would be harmful. But I learned and persevered and have been growing them ever since.

Note: For those unfamiliar with the term 'F1 hybrid', a brief explanation is offered. Sexual reproduction between two different plants

of the same genus results in a wide range of progeny, no two of which exhibit exactly the same characteristics. But it is possible using a process known as inbreeding to develop genetically pure parental lines. These parents, when crossed, will then yield seed that will produce offspring which are more or less identical in most characteristics. This is the F1 generation. The process of developing pure lines is a long one, six years or so, and the actual crosses are normally done by hand. The pollen from the staminate parent is collected manually and the pistillate flowers are then hand pollinated. While seed production is normally undertaken in countries where there is a ready source of cheap labour, seed produced in this way is considerably more expensive than seed which is open pollinated.

Author's note: Much of the information about Nonstop begonia culture, not all of which is presented here, was gleaned over the years in conversations with Ken Bosch, a good friend and excellent plantsman, who passed away earlier this year. This article is dedicated to his memory. 🐾

See page 97 for photos.

Osteospermum 101

by Jared VanBeveren

Osteospermum, also known as Cape Daisy, African Daisy, or Blue-eyed Daisy, originally come from South Africa. They were first propagated for commercial use in the floriculture industry 20-25 years ago. Osteospermum have become increasingly popular since their introduction, and there are as many as 70 varieties on the market today.[1] The flowers range in colour, and include many purples, pinks, yellows, whites, and bi-colours. Their petals also can have different shapes, from a flat, smooth petal to a dipped, spoon shaped petal. The plants themselves tend to have an upright habit, but there are a few varieties that have a more spreading habit.

Osteospermum prefer cool night temperatures (45-60° F) to bloom, and tend to stop flowering in the heat of mid summer when the night temperature gets above 60° F.[2] Plants will bloom again in late summer/early autumn when the night temperature once again falls below 60° F. There are notable exceptions that will not stop flowering in the high heat of summer. The blooms also have an interesting habit of closing up in low light conditions and at night, and then reopening in the morning. Osteospermum, as a rule, are also deer resistant.[3]

With so many commercially available varieties, it can be difficult to know which one to choose. Below I will discuss the most common varieties sold on the Prairies, and what characteristics set them apart from each other.

1. **Crescendo** series: This series is notable for its vigorous habit and large flower size. It is commonly grown in large containers or beds. It has three colours including orange, white, and primrose.[4]
2. **Serenity** series: One of the most uniform on the market, with excellent branching and a compact, mounded habit. It has nine different colours, including whites, purples, yellow, and two spoon-petal varieties.[5]
3. **Side** series: This series is especially cold-tolerant, which allows it to be outside earlier than standard varieties. It has five colours (white through purple), including two bicolors (white with purple and pink).[6]
4. **Soprano** series: An upright series that is more heat tolerant than standard varieties. The plants will eventually lose their blooms in the heat, but tend to go on blooming later into summer than standard

types. There are six colours (white through purple), including two spoon-petal varieties. This series is not a uniform one in terms of plant habit. 'Lilac Spoon' is the most vigorous. 'Compact Purple' and 'White' are 15–25 cm (6–10 in) tall; 'Vanilla Spoon' is the tallest at 30–60 cm (12–24 in).[7]

5. **Summertime** series: This series is characterized by a wide colour range, excellent branching and upright habit. There are twenty colours in this series, with many unique and unusual bi-colours. This series is not particularly heat tolerant and will lose its blooms by mid summer.[8]

6. **Symphony** series: One of the most popular series on the market today, these spreading osteospermum come in five colours, including a solid orange. They are also very heat tolerant, and will not stop blooming all summer. The blooms will, however, shrink somewhat compared to their spring bloom size.[7]

7. **Tradewinds/Tradewinds Trailing** series: This series is noted for its ability to flower in higher temperatures than standard varieties, as well as its compact growth habit. The Trailing varieties have a spreading habit which includes a unique spreading purple colour. There are a total of eleven colours in this series including Terra Cotta and a solid yellow.[9]

All osteospermum need to be grown in a well drained soil, as the roots do not like to sit in soggy media. Do not over-water as osteospermum can be susceptible to root rot. Also, do not allow soil to become parched, as this can cause the plant to go into a dormant phase to conserve energy. In this phase, the plant will lose its top growth and will appear dead, until water is reintroduced.[10] Osteospermum also need to be grown in full sun to part shade lighting conditions. A general purpose fertilizer is recommended once a month for flowering plants in order to promote blooming.[10] Pinching is not generally necessary for the above mentioned series, but can be used to shape a more compact, bushy plant in late summer.

Availabilty, as well as other series-specific growing details, can be explored by speaking to a garden centre in your area. 🦌

Endnotes:

1 www.umass.edu/umext/floriculture/fact_
   sheets/specific_crops/newcrops.html
2 www.ecke.com/datasheets/ff_ffx_sunsca-
   pedaisy.html
3 www.marigoldnurseries.com/pdf/deerre-
   sistant.pdf
4 www.ecke.com/Search200404/Variety_
   Results.asp
5 www.ballhort.com
6 www.ecke.com/Search200404/Variety_
   Results.asp
7 www.provenwinners.com
8 www.dummenusa.com
9 www.syngentaflowersinc.com/default.
   aspx?tabid=28&pid=35-851
10 davesgarden.com/guides/articles/view/1099/

See page 93 for photos.

Dahlias for the Prairies

by John Rempel

John Rempel is a well known gardener in the Charleswood area of Winnipeg. He is interested in lily hybridization and is the current president of the Manitoba Regional Lily Society.

Dahlias, in spite of their beauty, do not have a prominent place in most of our prairie gardens. This may be because of unfamiliarity with dahlia cultivation or the fact that dahlia tubers must be dug and stored for the winter months. A glance into a good dahlia catalogue with its hundreds of different cultivars of varying form and colour can be enough to tempt a novice to try their hand at adding this flower to their plant collection.

The genus dahlia is native to the highlands of Mexico as well as parts of Central America. There are approximately 35 recognized species in existence. Dahlias did not make their appearance in Europe until 200 years after they were originally discovered by the Spanish. In 1789, the botanist Vincent Cervantes shipped some dahlia seeds to the Royal Botanical Gardens in Seville, Spain. Botanist Antonio Jose Cavanilles who was in charge of the gardens, named the genus *Dahlia* in honour of a Swedish botanist Andreas Dahl who had died two years previous. From these seeds, 3 new plant forms were named: *D. pinnata*, *D. rosea* and *D. coccinea*. Plants were exchanged throughout Europe starting in the early 1800's.

Until 1804, there was very little variability in the dahlias, but after some new seeds were added, there was a dramatic change in form and colour. The new dahlias were so easy to hybridize that by 1936, there were over 14,000 recognized cultivars.

Cultivation

Dahlias enjoy a well drained site of friable fertile soil with lots of organic matter. They like a sunny location but enjoy some shade in the hot afternoon.

In early spring, it is time to purchase new stock, or if you have saved your own tubers from the previous year, to check out your tubers to see if they have survived the winter. This is the time to divide your clumps into individual tubers or check your tubers if you divided them in the fall. Tubers must be firm and free of rot. Each tuber must have an 'eye' which is attached to the base of the stem. This is the beginning of the new sprout. For early bloom, the tubers can be planted in flats or in 6 inch pots by mid-April. The tubers

should be watered very sparingly as they will rot if kept too wet. Leave the neck of the tuber exposed.

Tubers can be planted directly outdoors when the soil warms up to 12° C (55° F) and about a week before the last frost free date. Started plants should be planted out about the same time as tomatoes. Plant the dahlias two to three feet apart depending on the type of dahlia. The miniature dahlias can be spaced closer and can be left to multiple stems. Dig a hole six inches deep, place the tuber flat with the eye facing up. Cover with 8 cm (3 in) of soil. If the soil is moist, no further water is required until good growth starts.

As the plant grows, progressively fill up the rest of the hole with good soil. If there are multiple sprouts, leave only the strongest one. Dahlias must be strongly staked and tied or they will break from our occasional wind storms. Place a strong stake into the ground at the head of the tuber before it is planted. Now is a good time to scatter a handful of low nitrogen slow release fertilizer around the base of the plant. Later in the season, when the buds begin to show, an application of a fertilizer higher in phosphorus and potash can be added to facilitate larger blooms. To produce healthy growth, the plants should be given a good weekly soaking, or in hot weather, soak often enough to keep the soil moist.

For large quality blooms, pinch out the growing tip of the plant

Dahlia tuber with 'eyes' showing

after it has about five sets of leaves. This encourages lateral growths from the leaf axils and results in fewer but larger blooms. When the buds appear in clusters of three, disbud (pinch-off) the two outside buds when they are quite small. This will give you one quality bloom per lateral stem. Of course if you desire lots of bloom, let nature take its course. Show-quality dahlias are produced by disbudding (pinching lateral buds to leave the terminal ones), but leaving all of the buds will provide greater garden beauty.

Dahlias have the same pests as other plants in your garden, mostly aphids and thrips when the weather turns hot and dry. At one time dahlia growers resorted to pesticides but today a stream of cold water may deter the pests. In severe cases you may need to resort to whatever your local garden centre suggests.

Due to a lack of proper storage facilities, most gardeners discard their plants after the first hard frost. If you have a storage facil-ity where the temperature can be kept at 4–10° C (40-50° F), you may want to try to store them over the winter. After the first hard frost cut the tops about a foot above the ground and wait a few days for the tubers to harden. Dig the clumps carefully and wash off the excess soil. Leave them in a cool dry place for a while to harden off the skins before storage. Each grower has their own storage techniques, but I have found that simply leaving the clumps whole until spring and stor-ing them in a garbage bag in a cool place worked well for me. Check the tubers for rotting and excess mois-ture during the winter.

The American Dahlia Society (www.dahlia.org) has a very good web site for gardeners wishing more information on this unique flower. A good source of quality Canadian grown dahlias is Ferncliff Gardens (www.fern-cliffgardens.com) in Mission, BC. 🐞

See page 98 for photos.

The language of flowers, sometimes called floriography, was a Victorian-era means of communication in which various flowers and floral arrangements were used to send coded messages, allowing individuals to express feelings which otherwise could not be spoken.

Dahlia = Elegance and Dignity

Fuchsia
by Sue McLeod

Sue McLeod and husband Rob run Glenlea Greenhouses just south of Winnipeg, MB. They also teach courses on plant propagation and greenhouse construction.

Ask any child that comes into the greenhouse what is their favourite flower that they see—quite often it is the fuchsia. Colourful sepals with contrasting petals often remind them of ballerina tutus, with the stamens coming out of the bottom of the petals acting as legs. Flowers fallen from the baskets above never go wasted as their little hands scoop them up as treasures to take home. Unfortunately, many gardeners consider the plants difficult to grow, without even trying them first, simply because the flowers look exotic, assuming there must be a degree of difficulty that goes into growing them. On the contrary, given the proper growing conditions, fuchsias will reward you with a summer of profuse blooms, and to those willing to try, they will overwinter in the home for the following year. As an added bonus, they will attract hummingbirds and butterflies to your garden. Not a spring goes by that my greenhouse doesn't have hummingbirds darting from one fuchsia to the next while waiting for the outdoor flowers to begin blooming.

Fuchsias thrive in areas with morning sun and protection from the heat of the day. Provide soil that doesn't dry out excessively, but with sufficient drainage to prevent it becoming waterlogged. Often fuchsias will wilt in the heat of the sun, and gardeners assume that they are dry and over-water them. This only compounds the problem causing the roots to rot off, resulting in worse wilting. Always check the moisture level of the soil before watering. Sometimes moving the plant to a more shaded area is the best solution. When planting fuchsia in baskets or containers, use three or more around the edge of the pot, and one in the centre to avoid a bald spot in the middle. Multiple plants in the basket or container require frequent feeding, with weekly

Windchime Pink/White
(Proven Winners)

applications of liquid general purpose fertilizer a must for continuous blooming plants.

The key to having the plant bloom for the entire season is to deadhead. Once the flower has dropped, a green seedpod will remain and mature to a purple berry like fruit. It is essential that routine deadheading occur to encourage new buds to form. Like many flowering plants, once seed is produced, the plant has met its objective and will not produce many more flowers. Few varieties will drop both the seedpod and the flower at the same time. 'Lena' is a variety that is one of my favourites for this very reason. Keeping the plant seed free will give you more blooms.

When dead-heading your plants, take the time to check the undersides of the leaves for pests. Common insect pests of the fuchsia include aphids, whiteflies and spider mites. Treatment with insecticidal soap is effective, and when combined with maintaining proper moisture and feeding levels, the plant should be able to overcome the infestation.

After a rewarding summer of blooms, it is often hard to dispose of the fuchsia in the fall. The plant must be brought in before the first fall frost. As difficult as it may be, trim the plant to two thirds its size, removing new growth and blooms. The change in the location from outside to inside will be traumatic for the plant resulting in bloom drop, so it is just as easy to remove them before bringing the plant indoors. Inspect the plant to see if it is harbouring any insects, especially on the underside of the leaves. Remove any dead leaves from the soil surface, scraping away 2½ cm (1 in) of the soil on the top and replacing it with new soil to reduce the chance of harbouring any insects in the soil. Spray with insecticidal soap, or if possible, submerge the plant in a pail of the solution so all plant surfaces are treated.

Place the plant in strong light. Place moist pebble trays under the plant in the winter to raise the humidity. Keep the soil moist but not wet and resume feeding at one-half the rate once new growth has begun. Remove any dead or dying stems and all seed pods that may have gone unnoticed. Watch for insects carefully, with spider mites being the most probable in the dry conditions of a winter home. Fuchsias will not bloom in the home unless they have at least 12 hours of light per day to initiate blooming. Once danger of frost is past in the spring, gradually harden your plant off before placing it outside for yet another rewarding year of ballerina flowers.

Recommended varieties
- Swingtime – red and white; trailing
- Dark Eyes – red and purple; trailing
- Lena – pink and purple; trailing
- Windchime series – white, pink, red, purple; upright
- Winston Churchill – red and purple; upright 🌿

See page 99 for photos.

The Other Potato Plants
– Ipomoeas and Solanums
by Carla Hrycyna

Over the past few years, one particular plant, Ipomoea (Potato Vine), has been making headway into gardens and container plantings. Yet, twenty five years ago, if someone were to ask a greenhouse attendant for a 'potato plant', they were quickly given directions to the 'hard goods' section where seed potatoes ranging from russets to reds were located.

Times have changed! The potato plant, as with many other variety of plants have common names that may pertain to a multitude of plants, be it a perennial, annual, tropical or vegetable. Today's response to the query is: "Which annual vine would you prefer, *Solanum jasminoides* or the cascading planter type, *Ipomoeas batatas*?"

Both 'potato' plants serve strong structural patterns in the annual garden.

Ipomoea batatas (Convolvulaceae family), or sweet potato vines, consist of selections of leaf shape and colour. Grown as ornamental plants, the potato vines are used in both residential and commercial landscapes, either in containers or gardens. Fleshy roots give way to a vigorous growth habit. The sweet potato vine functions as a cascading plant when placed in containers; while creeping along the ground when planted in the garden. The leaf shape changes from one variety to another with spade (heart) leaves, or palmate- lobed leaves. Colour choices range from chartreuse (green), to bronze, to deep purple to variegated green and white with pink. It is difficult to

Ipomea Sweet Caroline
(Carla Hrycyna)

choose a colour. I am impressed by the strength of the colour that the Sweet Potato plant gives in the garden. To be honest, I have not tried to be creative with cooking the yam-like tubers to see if they are truly 'potatoes'.

Ipomoeas should be placed outdoors when frost free. It should be noted that these plants are quick to collapse when touched by frost or near frost conditions. These plants favour full sun to part shade and are a great plant to use in various locations. Their cascading vines may be left to ramble on their own, or occasional 'pinching' of leaders may be done to promote compact growth on more vigorous varieties. Most people think of Ipomoeas as being strictly foliage plants, however, given optimal growing conditions, they will produce 2½–5 cm (1–2 in) blooms. My own Ipomoea 'Sweet Caroline Purple' has lovely lavender blooms held delicately above the foliage.

Increased use of structural plants in gardens and containers such as annual grasses, foliage cascading plants *Hedera* (a.k.a English Ivy), *Muehlenbeckia* (a.k.a wire plant), and Coleus, along with Ipomoeas are viewed favourably for their low maintenance. [Note – these are just a sampling of foliage plants available to the gardener.]

Ipomoea varieties include: *Ipomoea batatas* 'Blackie', *Ipomoea batatas* 'Margarita', *Ipomoea batatas* 'Tricolour', *Ipomoea Sweet Caroline* 'Bronze', 'Purple', 'Red'. Look for a new selection in the Sweet Caroline series – 'Sweet Talk Purple' (palmate leaves with deep purple black colouring).

Solanum jasminoides (or *Solanum laxum*) commonly known as the 'potato vine' is an annual plant when grown in the prairies. In southern United States, the potato vine can be an invasive plant—not so in the Prairies. Its lacy leaf structure is a complement to the delicate cluster of white blooms (terminal panicles). This is usually composed of five to seven individual, 2-3 cm (¾-1 in) wide blooms with yellow stamens. I prefer the white blooms, though it is also available in soft blue. The slightly scented clusters held gracefully away from the leaves dance lightly in the breeze. Its vigorous growth habit makes it a favourite for annual screening purposes, arbors or trellises. With perfect growing conditions, the potato vine can reach between 3½-6 m (12-20 ft) in length. I recommend pinching new plants slightly to encourage branching so as to optimise coverage. Try combining *Solanum jasminoides* with a large leaf climber such as Morning Glory for a striking effect.

If I have piqued your curiosity for this plant, I am glad. Plant an *Ipomoea* if you have never done so before, and be rewarded with a bountiful display of colourful foliage. 🪴

See page 99 for photos.

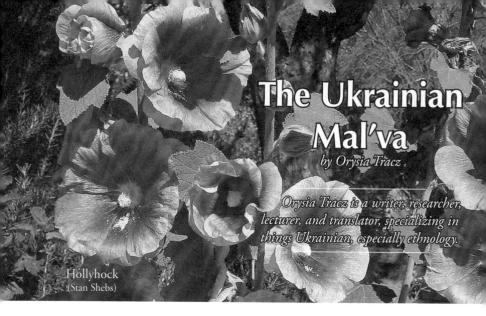

The Ukrainian Mal'va
by Orysia Tracz

Orysia Tracz is a writer, researcher, lecturer, and translator, specializing in things Ukrainian, especially ethnology.

Hollyhock
(Stan Shebs)

If you travel through the Ukrainian countryside today, you cannot help but notice the lushness of the gardens surrounding each house in the village. The fruit trees, the kalyna (viburnum, high-bush cranberry), the sunflowers, phlox, roses, marigolds, calendula, and other traditional flowers – all create the idyllic but real picture of the beauty of the Ukrainian village – what Taras Shevchenko described as "a village (as beautiful) as a pysanka (Ukrainian Easter egg)."

The one flower that grows right at the walls of the house is the hollyhock, the *mal'va*. Whether in paintings, photographs, or other images of a village house, that row of hollyhocks is both ubiquitous and an essential presence. The mal'va symbolizes beauty and youth, and is an integral part of the village landscape. It has a variety of regional names – *mal'va*, *ruzha*, *rozha*, and *kalachyky* or *kolachyky*. The first, of course, is the same as the Latin name for the

plant (with a soft "L"). *Ruzha* and *rozha* could also be the name of the rose as well as the hollyhock, but very often, the latter is called *ruzha*. The the name *kalachyky/kolachyky* is the diminutive of *kalach/kolach*, the round Ukrainian ritual bread. The flower is a circle, as is the seed pod, plump and round, like a *kolach*. And the root word is *kolo* – circle.

One must be careful with folk names of plants, because the same name can mean a completely different grass or flower a few villages away. In general, this may not matter, but when it comes to medicinal or poisonous plants, it can matter a great deal. Botanist Natalia Ossadcha-Janata compiled *Plant Names in Ukrainian Vernacular* (collected in 1927-1939 in Ukraine) (New York: Ukrainian Academy of Arts and Sciences in the Unites States, 1973). This book lists the Ukrainian names for 810 plant species. For example, *Babka* or *babky* (pl.) can be the name for five to eight completely different plants. *Krivavnyk* and similar names involving the root word for blood (usually astringents) can represent about eleven plants. Well, as long as they stop the bleeding.....

In general, the word *ruzha* denotes the various kinds of *mal'va*, as well as the rose, but in one particular village in Vinnytsia Province, *ruzha* is the *Gerum rivale*.

And when *ruzha* is mentioned in folk songs, not always would you know what flower it is supposed to be. *Malva neglecta* is the *malva zvychaina*, or ordinary malva. *Malva pusilla, rotundifolia* is *kalachyky kruhlosysti* or *dribnen'ki* (round-leaved or fine-leaved). *Malva crispa* is *kalachyky kucheriavi* (curled-leaved). *Malva mauritiana* is *dzindziver*. *Malva silvestris* is *kalachyky lisovi* (forest malva). *Malva excisa* is *kalachyky zayachi* (rabbit) or *kalachyky virizni* (cut-out-leaved. Again, an example of name variation, *dzindziver* is *Malva mauritiana* in Sumy Province (easternmost Ukraine) and *Malva silvestris* in Kam'ianets'-Podil'skyi Province (in the centre of Ukraine).

A few years ago, when I was presenting the lecture *Baba Was Right All Along: Ukrainian Folk Medicine*, I received a call from Central Manitoba from a woman who was trying to recall what a particular plant was called. She remembered it from childhood and her mother and baba had used it medicinally for particular stomach problems. She described it generally as something like a small hollyhock, and said that the juice from the plant was "gooey" or *slyz'ke* in Ukrainian. Turns out *slyz* or *slyzh* is the folk name for the common mallow, *Malva ssylvestris*, and the Ukrainian word for slippery is *slyz'ke*. The mallow contains mucilage, helpful in coating inflamed intestines, as does its close relative *Althea officinalis*.

The leaves, flowers, and roots of the various wild malvas are used as antitoxins and help in bronchial infections, as well as being a diuretic. To enhance the therapeutic strength of the flowers and leaves of the mallow or malva, it is often combined with the flowers of the wild poppy, buckwheat, and coltsfoot. Externally, an infusion of the leaves and flowers is used for burns and other skin ailments, and for gingivitis. As a prophylaxis, young leaves of the mallow are used in salads. Often the malva is used interchangeably with the related *Althea* for healing.

A poignant, moving song is the *Ballad about the Malva*, not a folk song, but one composed by Ukrainian song writer and poet Volodymyr Ivasiuk. In this case, he composed the melody, and Bohdan Hura the lyrics. Hura must have been prescient in writing these lyrics. Ivasiuk, a young doctor, was also a musician and award-winning composer who wrote songs inspired by Ukrainian folk music and folk lore, including flowers. His most famous song, Chervona

Ruta (The Red Rue) is still sung often, and is practically an anthem. He was a patriot who was opposed to the Russian Communist occupation of Ukraine and all it entailed. Songs must be a dangerous weapon (and, in history, they have been), because on April 24, 1979 in Lviv he was taken into a car awaiting him near his residence and was not seen again. His body was discovered in woods near Lviv on May 24, hanging from a tree, with evidence of a beating and torture. Sprigs of *kalyna* (viburnum – a symbol of Ukraine) were stuck into cuts on his body. The official KGB verdict was "suicide." His funeral transformed into a massive demonstration, and his grave was covered with an enormous mound of flowers. During the night, authorities removed the flowers, but the next day, more flowers replaced them. This continued for months. Authorities also tried to hide the tomb at Lychakiv Cemetery from foreign visitors, often giving wrong directions or saying it was not there. After Ukraine achieved independence, a monument was erected on his grave, and is a must-visit site for anyone visiting Lviv. The bouquets of fresh flowers are always there, thirty years after his death.

"The malvy (plural of malva) are asleep near the house, and the moon is rocking them, and only mother is not asleep, awaiting me. Dear mother, don't wait for me, I will not return into our home again. The malva is growing out of my heart, and is blooming in blood. Do not cry, mother, you are not the only one, many malvy were sown by the war. They whisper to you in autumn, "Sleep, sleep." Some mothers have dear children, but my mother only has flowers (left). The lonely flowers at the window have fallen asleep long ago. Mother, when the sun rises, come outside. People will bow to you (honouring you). Walk through the field, and the malvy will touch your hands. Life is like a never-ending song. I will live in the malva for you. If I could not bring all that is good to you, please forgive me, forgive me….."

When you walk through neighbourhoods in prairie towns and cities, you will see the malvy standing guard along houses and garages. Just a guess, but more often than not the homes have a Ukrainian connection. 🌺

See page 100 for photos.

The language of flowers was a Victorian-era means of communication in which various flowers were used to send coded messages, allowing individuals to express feelings.

Hollyhock = Ambition

Cool Annuals

by Alfred G. Prins

Horticulturist, Parkland Nurseries & Garden Centre, Red Deer, AB

On the Canadian Prairies we have several "cool" days throughout our growing season and more particularly, at the beginning and end of each season. To achieve success in the garden despite these conditions, a number of points come to mind based on my many years of experience gardening in Central Alberta.

Cold Tolerant Plants

While we cannot call the ever popular pansy and its small cousin, Viola, perennials on the prairies, they are the toughest of annuals, and will actually occasionally overwinter when given good snow cover. There are, however, many other annuals that will sustain a few degrees of frost. These include Carnations, Dianthus, Snapdragons, Dusty Miller, Godetia, and Petunias. Pansies and Violas may be planted out as early as late April and the others listed above may be planted out in early to mid May. Most other annuals are best set out later in May or early June.

Toughen up your plants

Plants that are greenhouse grown are, of course, very tender and will not withstand freezing temperatures or scalding sunshine. Plants should be moved outside during the day and brought in during the night to 'condition' or 'acclimatize' them. This is also known as hardening them off. Any growing procedure that does not promote fast soft growth will help produce more durable plants. Using fertilizers high in nitrogen (the first number on the fertilizer package) and excessively warm growing temperatures will produce very soft plants. When setting your plants out for the first time to harden off, place them where they will be in the shade all afternoon.

Protective Measures

If you have hardened your plants off and have planted them out and frost is still imminent, some form of protection will be needed during frosty nights. The best covers are the double walled plastic covers that can be filled with water. The next best is to gently lay old blankets, sheets, or towels over the plants. Merely running a simple sprinkler over your plants while the plants are thawing in the morning after a night frost will ease the frost damage. Commercially available frost blankets are also excellent and can be doubled up for extra protection.

Gardening on the prairies can certainly be challenging with all the fickle weather we seem to get, but we can grow some amazing gardens here, and when we succeed, it truly is rewarding. ❧

See page 101 for photos.

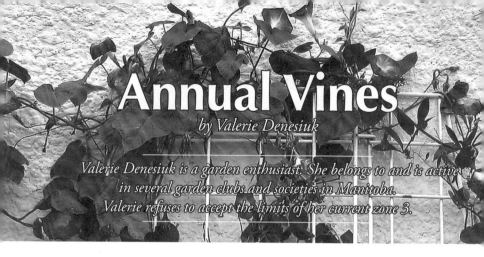

Annual Vines

by Valerie Denesiuk

Valerie Denesiuk is a garden enthusiast. She belongs to and is active in several garden clubs and societies in Manitoba. Valerie refuses to accept the limits of her current zone 3.

Vines can be some of the most wonderful plants garden enthusiasts have at their disposal. They are amazingly versatile, giving our landscapes a vertical component where trees and shrubs just won't do the job. Vines are easy to grow in flower beds, hanging baskets, window boxes or trellised planters. Vines may be planted alone or in combination with other annual or perennial vines. They provide a quick and inexpensive solution as an artistic focal point or to hide something unattractive.

Vines add a vertical dimension which can make small spaces seem larger. They can function to provide privacy with dense screening and cooling shade; all the while elevating delightful flowers to eye level for your enjoyment.

Most annual vines won't cling to brick or wooden walls, but you can use such climbing aids as twine, wire fences or trellises to support them. Planting climbing vines along chain link fences or light poles may soften the look of your landscape. Whether accenting pleasing architecture, or softening harsh structural lines, the colour, texture and height of vines provide limitless variety. Vines are also ideal for creating a natural screen for privacy and protection from sun and wind. Planting vines along a southern wall will keep the house cooler in summer. They also create an excellent habitat for birds, bees, and butterflies. Annual vines grow rapidly and can fill in temporarily for slower growing perennial vines.

Annual vines climb by twining around a support or by clinging with tendrils. Most annual vines grow rapidly to form an attractive mass of foliage and flowers. The more vigorous the vine, the heavier weight the twine or netting you'll need.

Annual vines can also be used as a form of a ground cover and will quickly blanket a problem slope or other area that is difficult to mow with colourful flowers. If your slope is difficult to plant, use a vine that will reseed itself, such as morning glories or cardinal climbers. Vines are excellent for tiny courtyards, yards or apartment balconies. Instant charm and colour can be added in any sized space by framing a door or window with a climbing vine, even on a string trellis.

Generally speaking, annual vines are easy to grow. Most do well in a sunny location with good quality, well drained soil. Plant your seeds according to the package directions, and keep them evenly moist until they germinate. After germination, you'll only need to water when the weather is extremely hot or dry. Have your trellises or other support in place when you plant your seeds. If you can't plant right next to the support, insert twigs into the soil next to the seeds to lead the vines to their intended support. If the vine can't find its support right away, it will waste time searching and reaching for something to grab on to.

Use fertilizers sparingly. Excess nitrogen will result in an abundance of dark green foliage and few flowers. Roots of annual climbers require little space; they need little care and have few insect or disease problems. Because their root systems are limited they are ideal for planters and containers.

Annual vines are ideal for introducing your children to the magic of gardening. Build a teepee of bamboo or fallen tree branches, and plant with scarlet runner beans or tall nasturtiums. Your children will enjoy their colourful (and edible) hideaway while learning about the wonders of nature. Kids love them because annual vines grow so quickly they can almost see them reach for great heights or stretch to new lengths. Because the seeds are large, kids can easily sow them with just a little help from adults.

Support Systems

If you don't have instant supports like a fence or trellis system already available, consider running twine from the ground to supports above, such as the eaves of roofs, or the side of a raised deck. Tent stakes can be used to anchor these in the ground. Vines can also be allowed to climb among branches of shrubs, or climb through that dead shrub or tree you have not yet removed, or simply on branches you have stuck in the ground.

Allow your creativity to flow! If you plan to make trellises, arbours, and other support structures, consider using: netting, twine, metal, PVC pipe, decay-resistant wood, and rustproof wire (such as plastic-coated or copper electrical wire). Structures should be placed far enough away from buildings to allow air circulation and should be positioned before vines are planted. Vines tend to flower mostly along the top of growth. Whereas vertical support works for most vines, a grid-style support will allow for greater spread and horizontal support of annual vines. Green vinyl netting or fencing is particularly valuable for this purpose because it disappears from view.

Most annual vines climb by using tendrils or by twining. Tendrils are slim, flexible stems or leaf modifications that can quickly wrap themselves around anything they come in contact with to support the vine for further growth. Tendrils curl because cells on one side of the stem grow faster than the other side—how much faster determines the tightness of the curl. Vines that have tendrils appreciate narrow horizontal supports. They also do well on netting or grids.

Twining vines wind their stems around any available support—usually in a clockwise direction. They need predominantly vertical supports as well as horizontal supports every 20–30 cm (8–12 in) for their side branches. Twining vines tend to have more vigorous growth habits than tendrilled vines and may need pruning.

Before planting an annual vine in a selected location, consider not just by the current need, but how you plan to use the space in the future. Many annual vines will reseed themselves and can continue in an area for many years after. The Morning Glory 'Grandpa Ott' is a good example from my own experience. A beautiful dark blue-purple with a pinkish star, I am still pulling seedlings almost 8 years after I replanted an area that Grandpa Ott originally occupied. Morning Glories, with their wide variety of colours, leaf shape and variegation, are one of the fastest growing vines. They and other annual vines should not go into compost unless you don't mind them all over your yard in the coming years. Some people call Morning Glories 'weeds' rather than wonderful because of this.

The same can be said about native vines such as wild cucumber.

Whereas there are many Heritage sweet peas, morning glories and other traditional annual vines that thrive in our temperate zone, look beyond these to the many other newer vines available on the market today. Seed catalogues and bedding plant outlets offer many new climbing vines such as passion flower, Mandevilla, or edible spinach. Yes, spinach! The new tender leaves of Malabar Spinach Vine (*Basella rubra*) are very edible. It provides an interesting climbing vine in shades of green with a purple tone, and flowers that resemble an upside down bunch of tiny grapes.

There are many vegetables that you can have climbing or hanging throughout your garden either alone or mixed in with your decorative flowering varieties. Many people have used peas, cucumbers, beans, and hops as not just tasty or useful crops, but as decoration in their gardens. One should also consider various squashes or gourds ie: Birdhouse gourds (*Cucurbita*), vegetable sponge (*Luffa cylindrical*), various zucchini or anything that reasonably can be put on a trellis or allowed to hang over an edge.

Exercise full freedom of expression regarding function, purpose and style in your landscape planning when annual vines are used as an option. In the following table, there are some specific suggestions but always read the seed package or information guide when considering any plant in your garden.

See page 102 for photos.

Annual Vines

Common Name	Botanical Name	Height m/ft	Comments
Vines That Grow Quickly			
common morning glory	*Ipomoea purpurea*	to 3m 10ft	Funnel shaped flowers from midsummer to fall; many different colours. Can self seed and become very full even in the first year.
cypress vine	*Ipomoea quamoclit*	2½–3m 8–10ft	Fine lacy leaves; star–shaped tubular red, pink and white flowers.
cardinal climber	*Ipomoea x multifida*	1¾–6m 6–20ft	Ferny foliage; twining; red trumpet–shaped flowers.
annual sweet pea	*Lathyrus odoratus*	–1¾m 2–6ft	Pea–type flowers; honey–orange blossom scent; grows best in cool weather. Picking blooms encourages more blooms through the summer. Growing various height types creates a wall of colour.
climbing nasturtium	*Tropaeolum majus*	1¼–1¾m 4–6ft	Twining; fragrant, edible flowers in red, brown, yellow and bicolour.
Great Cascade Wine Red,	*Lophospermum*	1½–2¼m 5–7ft	Newer to the market, can be used to climb or hang but does better as a climber. Tubular flower shows well alone or in combination.

Common Name	Botanical Name	Height m/ft	Comments
Tropical Tender Perennial Vines usually treated as Annual. Either started from seed or bought as a bedding plant. Some will develop seeds for saving.			
cup and saucer vine, cathedral bells	*Cobaea scandens*	3–6m 10–20ft	5 cm (2 in) reddish purple flower cups in green saucers; tendrils.
Chilean glory vine	*Eccremocarpus scaber*	3–4½m 10–15ft	Orange, red, pink, or yellow clusters of flowers from summer to fall.
moonflower	*Ipomoea alba*	3–6m 10–20ft	Fragrant white flowers from midsummer to frost, heart–shaped leaves.
sweet potato vine ornamental	*Ipomoea batatas*	1¼–2½m 4–8ft	Several cultivars; 'Tricolour' has light green, pink to cream variegated leaves. Trellis or hanging basket. Tuberous roots can be stored over winter.
purple hyacinth bean	*Lablab purpureus*	1¾–6m 6–20ft	Purple fragrant, pea–type flowers; purple bean-like pods grown as a food crop in the tropics.
Spanish flag, firecracker vine	*Mina lobata*	1¾–4½m 6–15ft	Red flowers fading to yellow and cream. Twines.
passion flower	*Passiflora incarnata*	4½–6m 15–20ft	Tendrils; very exotic looking purple and white flowers, but is now available in a variety of colours. e.g. red or purple.
purple bell vine	*Rhodochiton atrosanguineum*	to 3m 10ft	Tendrils; tubular, deep purple flowers; heart–shaped leaves. Climbs or hangs.
black–eyed Susan vine	*Thunbergia alata*	1–2¼m 3–7ft	Twining; orange, yellow, pink and white flowers with black eye.
canary creeper	*Tropaeolum peregrinum*	2¼–3m 7–10ft	Twining; bright yellow flowers; fringed petals and a green spur.
scarlet runner bean	*Phaseolus coccineus*	3–4½m 10–15ft	Scarlet pea–type flowers; purple pods; twining; edible beans.
Mandevilla	*Mandevilla´ amabilis* or x *Amoena*	3–6m 10–20ft	Usually white or pink flowers, funnel shaped up to 10 cm (4 in). Twines, likes moist soil, over-winter inside by cutting back stems and watering only enough to prevent drying out.

Common Name	Botanical Name	Height m/ft	Comments
Vegetables that can be used as vines. Can be combined with traditional flowering vines.			
Gourds	Various ie: Birdshouse (*Curcubita*)	1–2½m 3–8ft	Can be edible or ornamental depending on what type is used.
Tomatoes	Most indeterminate (grow tall and vine-like)	trim to 2 m/ 6ft for proper support	Rather than `caging' tomatoes try wrapping around the cage or onto a trellis. Many smaller varieties can be `tumbled' out of a window box or hanging basket.
Beans	Various and many	3–4½m 10–15ft	Various trellis, or bush type. Could hang.
Cucumbers	*Cucumis sativus*	pinch at 2m/6ft	Smaller varieties are best for a trellis.
Zucchini	*Cucurbita pepo*	pinch at 2m/6ft	Provide support if it grows large.
Malabar Spinach Vine	*Basella rubra*	1¾–2½m 6–8ft	Tender younger leaves tasty in salad.

In Memorium: Phyllis Pierrepont
March 1, 1918 – June 16, 2009

In June of 2009 Phyllis Pierrepont died. She was an ardent gardener, horticultural colleague and friend.

Phyllis came to the Swan River area of Manitoba as a child, but spent her adult life in the Lady Hubble district west of Bowsman, MB. Phyllis was a member of the Bowsman Horticultural Society, became a director for the Manitoba Horticultural Association, later serving on its executive. As a certified horticultural judge at exhibitions and horticultural shows and a much sought after speaker, she shared her knowledge and enthusiasm for horticulture.

In 1947 Phyllis was given a lily bulb, the beginning of a 60 year interest in lilies; growing, testing, hybridizing, lecturing and writing about lilies. That intensive interest led to serious study of other plants; annuals, perennials, vegetables and fruits. She would grow as many as 20 varieties of something like tomatoes or potatoes keeping records of their growth and production, germination, flowering, ripe fruit and amounts harvested

When the Prairie Garden Committee introduced the Prairie Garden Award for Excellence as a centennial, project Phyllis was the first recipient. She graciously received that and many other awards including a bursary in her honour from our own horticulture society for a U of Manitoba horticulture student. The Manitoba Regional Lily Society presented her with a meritorious award for her work in promoting the genus Lilium.

Phyllis Pierrepont is remembered and respected by teens and contemporaries, friends and gardeners for her contribution to horticulture, her friendship, kindness and generosity.

Swayed to Use Grasses
by Carla Hrycyna

Mention the use of grasses in the garden or landscape these days, and you will pique the curiosity of any gardener, novice or experienced.

This has not always been the case. It was not long ago that 'grasses' were thought of as the sodded areas of our homes, the wide open areas of parks, or the finely clipped areas surrounding the ball park. As a child, I was never infatuated with, nor interested in the aspect or purpose of these well maintained areas. Grassy lawns only served the purpose of giving siblings, friends and me a place to play.

As I grew up, lawns took on a more manicured look— actually the lawns were probably always cared for, it was 'I' who finally started to pay attention to this aspect.

This attention to detail is still practiced by the many homeowners who have manicured, lush green lawns. The difference from when I was younger to now, is that the 'garden' has changed! Previously, the traditional garden consisted of vegetables and a few flowers. Today's modern garden consists of large perennial and annual beds combined with various selections of ornamental shrubs, trees and coniferous selections. Amongst the collection of plants are 'ornamental' grasses – both perennial and annual.

Why are we driven to include grasses in our environment? It may be the low maintenance factor, the fact that grasses have limited disease and pest problems, or the diversity of grass structure that encourages us to transform our way of landscaping. We commonly use grasses in our ornamental settings, including annual plantings and container gardening.

I know that it is the soft plume held above the grass blades, the sound of wind rustling through the reeds, the gentle sway of the grass blades on a breezy day or the idea that these plants will enhance my garden in every season, that attracts my attention. Knowing that there is a grass variety that will grow in just about any type of soil and soil condition is an added benefit. We have not even mentioned the numerous varieties that possess different characteristics (varying heights, plant shape, seed head shape and colour, and growth habit). Whoever said "grass is just grass" – Boy! Were they wrong!

My goal is to give you insight into the realm of annual grasses. Highlighting a few varieties you may already know, or introducing you to some you have not come across yet will enable you to decide to venture into the use of annual grasses in your garden. Please note though, when I mention 'annual grasses', I feel like I am severely neglecting all of the wonderful perennial grasses hardy to our area. Perennial grasses, like *Calamagrostis* 'Karl Foerster' (Feather Reed Grass) and *Miscanthus sinensis* purpurascens 'Autumn Red' (Flame Grass) are widely used in the landscape environment, but can also be treated as an annual plant, as can many other perennial grasses.

Annual grasses, like perennial grasses, enhance a landscape setting with a strong vertical element as we see in *Panicum* (Switch Grass), *Miscanthus* (Maiden Grass), *Molinia* (Tall Moor Grass), and *Calamagrostis* (Feather Reed Grass).

Panicum virgatum 'Northwinds' – clumping type grass with a v-shaped upper habit with almost 2 m (6 ft) tall beautiful blue green stems gracing tan coloured panicles mid summer through fall.

Miscanthus sinensis 'Autumn Red' (Flame Grass) – greyish green foliage up to 1½ m (5 ft) tall in a clumping form of wide leaf blades, which turn red-orange in the late-fall with silver plumes. Truly beautiful!

Molinia arundinacea 'Skyracer' – (Tall Moor Grass) has a unique form with low mounded blade growth of .6–.9 m (2–3ft) with gracefully tall flowering inflorescence reaching 1.8–2.4 m (6–8 ft) tall.

Each of these perennial grasses is considered an 'annual grass' if planted in containers. I mention this as perennials will generally not over--winter in containers through our

prairie winters. The dramatic effect of their height make these worthwhile contenders for container planting, not just perennial plantings.

Saccharum ravennae a.k.a. Hardy Pampas Grass (formally known as *Erianthus ravennae*) Zone 5 is a towering grass known to reach 2.4 m (8 ft) tall or over. Large pink blooms turn silver in the winter, creating a beautiful winter accent.

A true annual grass with dramatic height would be *Cortaderia selloana* (Pampas Grass) 'White Feather' and "Pink Feather' that grow even taller than their perennial counterpart. 'White Feather' topping at 3.7 m (12 ft) and 'Pink Feather' at 3 m (10 ft) are equally as impressive planted in a full sun location. Perfect for pot or garden. The blades of this grass are sharp so be careful when touching. The plumes of these varieties are enormous.

Most annual grasses prefer to be planted in a full sun location, in an area of well-drained soils for optimal growth. You will even find that some grasses will tolerate part sun and even moister conditions. It is best to always know which grass suits your growing conditions.

It should be mentioned that grasses are classed into two groups, clumping or non-clumping. Clumping grasses are generally tufted or mounded grasses that do not venture far from their original planting area. Non-clumping grasses, however, creep outwards by rhizomes, being classified as 'fast spreading' or invasive. Generally, some of our perennial grasses fall into this category. Annual grass is just for one season, and the roots will perish over the winter months.

Annual tufted and mounding grasses suit container gardening very well. The *Carex* family (though truly a grass-like sedge) possesses both mounding and tufted types. The mounding types of *Carex commans* (Leatherleaf) 'Amazon Mist' and *Carex commans* (Leatherleaf) 'Bronco' grow to 25 cm (10 in) tall, spreading 36 cm (14 in) wide with arching blades. The only difference in these two is their colour, 'Bronco' being bronze brown, the other variegated light green. *Carex buchananii* 'Red Rooster' is a favourite with its red bronze foliage and curled tips giving it a unique appearance. This tufted plant is perfect in a container planting, especially for a fall season planter. *Isolepis cernua* 'Live Wire' (Fibre Optic Grass) is fun and funky with its soft cascading habit. The tip of each blade is lightly 'tipped' giving it the appearance of fibre optics. This plant is listed as a zone 4, so may need some protection.

Melinis nerviglumis 'Savannah' (Ruby Grass) is worth a mention with its blue green blades turning a beautiful purple red tint in the fall. The blades of grass top off at 25 cm (10 in) tall with silky pink tufted heads appearing in mid summer fading to white over the winter. This grass is a prime example of a panicle being used for cut or dried arrangements.

The most favoured annual grass used singly or in mass plantings has to be *Pennisetum setaceum* 'Rubrum' – Purple Fountain Grass. Definitely, 'Rubrum' is the darkest purple foliage grass with purple to pink plumes reaching 91–122 cm (36–48 in) tall. They are extremely fast growing for an annual grass.

Annual grasses mentioned above have gained in popularity often replacing the 'dracena' or commonly known 'spike' normally used as the central focus in our pots. There are other noteworthy grass-like annuals worth mentioning that give us the same look of grass. *Pennisetum glaucum* - Ornamental Millet has corn-like stalks of deep purple to burgundy. Ornamental millets range in height from ¾ m (2 ½ ft) tall to 1 ½ m (5 ft) tall depending on variety. Unique colour change occurs when pot-grown millet looks green with burgundy undertones to the leaf blades, which quickly turn to its burgundy colour when placed in a full sun location. The thick cattail-like plume of this pennisetum is favourable for cut flowers.

We have noted only a few of the numerous varieties of annual grasses that are available. We have seen the height variations, colour choices, and growth habits. Grasses should be at the top of the list for any garden. 🪶

See page 103 for photos.

Annuals for Shade

by Dorothy Dobbie

Begonia rex (Valerie Denesiuk)

Some of my earliest memories are associated with annuals, the ones that thrived in my grandmother's garden. She grew the old fashioned kind: pretty pansies, the lovely little bachelor's buttons, the dreamy cosmos, and the highly scented stocks. I remember the bees buzzing at ear level, the flowers of cosmos and bachelor buttons meeting my gaze at eye level. I was very young. Most of her flowers were grown in the hot prairie sun, but some, like the bachelor's buttons and the pansies, flourished in the cool, damp shade under an old Manitoba maple – they were my favourites.

Growing annuals in shade is a tricky business. There just are not that many varieties to choose from, especially if you love flowers. Not only that, but not all shade is equal.

In-ground shade under trees is really partial shade because the plants get filtered sun and many annuals will tolerate this. It's often called dappled shade and lets in a gentle light to which many plants respond well. Impatiens, coleus, begonia are typical 'shade' plants that require some sunlight but prefer it to be filtered.

Shade cast by buildings and fences is another matter because the shade is very dense and unless there is a period of day where plants get the benefit of direct sunlight for a few hours, very few will be able to thrive.

Light is not, however, the only consideration. Shade can be dry or moist. The soil can be acidic or alkaline, depending on what causes the shade. It is often these factors that determine what can be grown and what can't.

Dry shade is the most challenging. Very light, loamy soil can be amended with organics: leaf mold or compost. I like to add some coir, (dried coco husk) to help the soil retain water. It breaks down slowly and will hold three times its weight in moisture. If the soil is really impossible, perhaps laced with tree roots that are competing for water resources, an alternative would be to sink a pot into the ground filled with your favourite moisture-loving coleus or impatiens.

Shade that is heavy and wet can impose its own limitations, but the solution is the same as for dry shade. Add organics and if that doesn't work, plant in containers set in the shade.

In spite of the challenges, there is one benefit to shade: many of the blue flowers grow in shade or part shade.

Browallia speciosa is one plant that is happy in fairly deep shade and still produces the prettiest little blue star-shaped flowers (it comes in white, too, but this colour is not so striking). Browallia is a small, 15-cm (6-inch), mounded plant with clear green leaves. It's a member of the potato family (*Solanaceae*) with its origins in South America. It likes a rich moist soil, so if your shade area is dry, you might want to grow it in a pot and put the pot in the shade.

Another blue plant for shade is *Myosotis sylvatica,* the unforgettable forget-me-not, that happy little denizen of the woodland whose cheery blue flowers sparkle like tiny lights on the woodland floor. It is the most commonly grown forget-me-not and technically is a biennial, but is often grown as a hardy annual. Their seeds attach to clothing or to the fur of passing animals so they travel quickly, but a carpet of forget-me-nots in early spring is not a bad thing. This is a plant that likes a well-drained, loamy soil.

The best flowering plant for a hanging basket in heavier shade is fuchsia, which needs less light than begonia or impatiens. Fuchsia is really a perennial in milder climates and it can handle a wide variety of conditions. While fuchsia can over winter indoors, it is usually infested with aphids or other crawlies which you may prefer to avoid.

Rex begonia foliage comes in such fantastic colours and shapes that their flowers are almost too much. Don't worry, though. They probably won't flower unless you take them inside to over winter, which they do very well.

Annual lobelia is really a shade-loving plant that prefers cool conditions just as do pansy and viola. Lobelia also likes evenly moist conditions.

Torenia fournieri, or wishbone flower (also known as blue wings) is another small plant, growing up to 30 cm (12 inches) tall, that appreciates shade. The blue, mauve or white flowers that have a spot of yellow in their throat resemble small orchids. Torenia is a member of the *Scrophulariaceae* family as are snapdragons and foxglove.

If you want to increase your shade-tolerant flowering annuals list, you may be surprised to learn that sweet alyssum (*Lobularia maritima*), nasturtium *(Tropaeolum)*, *Nicotiana*, *Dianthus* and bells of Ireland (*Moluccella*) all handle shade to partial shade very well.

The list of plants known for their foliage rather than flowers includes: caladium, dusty miller, English ivy, grape ivy, most of the Swedish ivies (*Plectranthus*) and the polka dot plant (*Hypoestes phyllostachya)* and of course, the shade-tolerant coleus.

A lot has changed since I met the flowers eye-to-eye in my grandmother's garden, not the least of which is the wide choice in annuals today. Even in the shade, there's room for a lot more bloom in the prairie garden.

We are so blessed to live in these wonderful times. 🐜

See page 103 for photos.

Biennials
by Ed Czarnecki

Ed Czarnecki, (BSA, Sc) retired as a cereal breeder from Agriculture and Agri-Food Canada. Some of his interests include perennial hybridizing, gardening, travelling, photography and study of native flora.

Evening Primrose
(Danny Steaven)

Biennials are basically two year plants, growing a short rosette or tap root the first year and then sending up a flowering stalk and setting seed in the second year before ceasing all physiological activity in the fall and drying up. Some examples include hollyhock, dianthus, foxglove, evening primrose, parsley, beets, carrots, lettuce, Swiss chard and some weeds such as common burdock, hemlock, biennial wormwood, caper spurge, and biennial thistles including musk, plumeless and bull thistle.

Evening Primrose
Oenothera biennis

Evening Primrose is a native biennial North American plant generally found east of the Rockies extending to the Atlantic and may be known by common names such as Fever plant, Sundrops, Suncups, Common Evening primrose, Seabish, King's cureall, etc.

It grows by roadsides, railway banks and waste places in dry open soils, sandy locations, meadows and undisturbed fields. The plants are fairly tall often ranging from 0.3–1.5 m (1–5 ft) or more in height. The stem is erect, soft, hairy, reddish in colour and branching with alternative leaves. Leaves are produced in a tight rosette in the first year and spirally on the stem in the second year. The leaves are rough, hairy, lanceolate in shape, from 5–20 cm (2–8 in) long and are lemon scented. The taproot is elongated, fibrous and yellow on the outside and whitish within. The flower spikes grow on auxiliary branches all along the stalk. The flower is about 2.5–5 cm (1–2 in) in diameter and bears four petals that are pale-yellow in colour. The inflorescence opens in the evening and closes up during the day, hence the name, 'Evening Primrose'. The open flowers emit a strongly scented fragrance which attracts pollinating moths. The resulting fruit is an oblong 2–4 cm (3/4-1 1/2 in) capsule which contains numerous, 1-2 mm (3/64–3/32 in) long tiny reddish seeds.

Evening Primroses are a popular ornamental plant in gardens. For propagation the seeds can be sown directly in a dry well-drained garden soil (preferably sandy loam) in an open area that is sunny to partial shade. The plants are fairly drought tolerant.

Foxglove
Digitalis purpurea

Foxglove is an attractive single stemmed herbaceous biennial plant with large and showy flowers that performs well in shade and cooler moist climates. It is a native of Western Europe, the Mediterranean and northwest Africa and has naturalized in these countries as well as in North America. As in similar biennials, the leaves are spirally arranged in the first year forming a compact ground level rosette. The flowering stem develops in the second year extending from 1–2 m (3.3–6.6 ft) tall and bears a one-sided spike of a showy elongated cluster of tubular nodding flowers (about 5 cm/2 in long) of purple, pink, rose, yellow cream or white colour. The inside of the corolla may have purple and white spots or streaks. The flowering period is early summer with additional stems developing later during the season. The fruit is a capsule which splits open at maturity to release numerous tiny seeds (0.1–0.2 mm/.004–.008 in). They are spread by wind and water and can remain viable in the soil for up to five years. Foxglove, which only reproduces by seed, does best in a moist acidic soil containing generous amounts of organic matter.

Foxglove is usually treated as a biennial where the seed is sown in late summer or fall and flowering occurs in the following spring and summer. Seeds should not be covered, germinating best at 20–27° C (68–80° F) and exposed to light. Under favourable conditions, Foxglove will self-seed. This biennial species is suitable for shady borders and flower beds and adds a vertical dimension to flower beds containing ferns, columbine or meadow rue. Foxglove will tend to naturalize in a partly shaded or wooded setting but is not considered invasive. Hummingbirds and bees are frequent visitors to this species.

Though originally a source of important heart medication (cardiac glycosides) all parts of the plant are extremely toxic, thus deer or rabbits will not consume foxglove. Several important pharmaceutical drugs such as digitalis and digoxin are derived from this plant.

A hybrid perennial foxglove was developed by the late Dr. Frank Skinner and named 'Dropmore Yellow'.

Common Hollyhock
Alcea rosea

Hollyhocks are native to the Orient but are grown world-wide and even though they are traditionally biennial, there are also annual and perennial forms.

Hollyhocks are attractive vertical-effect accent plants in the background of a border or planted against a fence or wall. The leaves are heart shaped and rough textured with flowers up to 10 cm (4 in) across unfurling as buds at the base of the stalks and progressing towards the top, producing a summer long display. The plants tend to self-sow and seedlings may differ from the parent flower. Flowers may be single, double or semi-double and come in yellow, white, rose, purple, pink red, lavender and almost black colours. The five petals of the flower have a crepe like structure and may be fringed or ruffled. Time of bloom ranges from summer to early autumn. Some of the older strains may grow to 3.5 m (11 ft) tall while more modern hybrids range from 0.5–2 m (1.6–6½ ft) and 0.3 m (1 ft) wide.

Seeds are generally sown in summer (6–9 mm/ ¼–3/8 in deep) and transplanted to a permanent location early the following spring, however, some varieties may bloom the first season. After flowering is complete the stalks can be cut and the daughter plants separated before replanting to perpetuate the mother plant. Hollyhocks prefer a well drained humus rich soil.

Early Scorpion Grass
Myosotis verna Nutt.

Spring or Early Scorpion Grass or White-Forget-Me-Not, a member of the Boraginaceae family, is a native biennial wildflower extending from southern British Columbia to Ontario and is also found in the northern and eastern United States. The name *Myosotis* comes from "mys" for mouse and "ous" for ear referring to the short soft leaves of some species.

This plant is generally not branched or branches occasionally with stems that are light green, terete (cylindrical and tapering) or angular and covered with long white hairs. The 1 to 5 cm long alternate leaves are light green, oblong or oblanceolate with rounded tips, smooth and ciliate along the margins and generally hairy on the upper and lower surfaces. The leaves are mainly sessile (stalkless) against their stems and each leaf has a prominent central vein while the lowest leaves taper to petiole-like structures along the stem.

The central and any upper lateral stems end in elongated racemes of small white flowers with each raceme having about 8 to 24 flowers. The flowers bloom toward the tip of each raceme, where it is typically curved like a scorpion's tail. Individual flowers are 3 mm across and consist of a white corolla with 5 rounded lobes, a hairy calyx with 5 lanceolate sepals, 5 inconspicuous stamens and a pistil. Flowering extends from mid-spring to early summer and lasts about 2 months. The racemes become extended as their dry ovoid fruits develop, with each fruit bearing 4 seeds. This species reproduces by reseeding itself. The hairy fruits can cling to the fur of mammals and clothing of humans thus helping to distribute the seed to new locations.

The root system of this species consists of a tap root with secondary fibrous roots.

Habitats include open woodlands, areas along woodland paths, railway embankments, sand prairies, fields and roadside embankments. This wildflower may occur in barren areas with little ground vegetation, commonly where there is a history of disturbance and occasionally it may be found in damper areas.

Honesty (Money Plant)
Lunaria annua
Honesty is a tall (height 30–100 cm/1–3 ft) hairy-stemmed biennial plant native to the Balkans and southwest Asia and naturalized throughout Europe, North America and parts of Asia. The genus Lunaria is derived from luna, the moon and reflects the shape of the seed pods. Honesty is an easy to grow plant that is called by different common names including Dollar plant, Penny Flower, Silver Dollars, Moonwort and Bolbonac. Honesty is grown for its fruit called silicles, that are ornamental when dried. The green outer covering peels off to reveal the silvery translucent "silver coins". The hairy strong-stalked stem elongates in early spring growing to a height of 50–100 cm (20–40 in) in its second year. Leaves are initially produced in pairs and are alternately arranged along the stem. The chordate (heart shaped) and acuminate (tapering) leaves are finely or coarsely serrated and of a medium to bright green colour in the spring and summer but darken in the fall.

The four petalled, bright, fragrant flowers bloom in early spring and summer and are usually purple or white, developing in groups at the top of the vertical main stem and branches. This species is self-fertile and is pollinated by visiting bees, flies, moths and butterflies, the latter of the Lepidoptera family.

The green seedpods are large, circular and flattened and are securely attached to the stem.

The seeds are also large, firmly compressed in two rows, and take on a purple colouration while ripening. When mature the outer cases and seeds fall away leaving the intermediate membranes still attached to the plants. A flat, thin-walled oval and translucent silicula (seed-head) is formed leaving "Silver Penny" which is used in floral arrangements.

The plant readily seeds itself freely around the garden and being well adapted to a temperate climate, will grow in most fertile soils. The fatty acid composition of the oil derived from the seeds may potentially be suitable for the production of high temperature lubricants and possibly for some pharmaceutical applications.

Sweet William
Dianthus barbatus
Sweet William is the common name for the barbatus species of Dianthus, a favourite flowering plant that is native to the mountains of southern Europe extending from the Pyrenees, east to the Carpathians and the Balkans with

a disjunct (separate) variety found in northeastern China, Korea and southern Russia. Of the two varieties, *Dianthus barbatus* var. *barbatus* from southern Europe has leaves being up to 2 cm (³/4 in) wide while the variety *Dianthus barbatus* var. *asiaticus* found in Northeastern Asia has slender leaves not over 1 cm (3/8 in) wide. Dianthus was one of the earliest plants cultivated by man primarily for ornamental purposes, however, it was also used to flavour wines in France and Spain. It is also said to be the first plant on which an entire book was written.

Sweet William is an herbaceous biennial or short-lived perennial plant growing from 30–75 cm (12–30 in) tall with tapered leaves being opposite, simple, mostly linear and often strongly glaucous greygreen to blue-green from 4–10 cm (1½–4 in) long and 1–2 cm (3/8–³/4 in) wide. Single or double forms of up to 30 flowers are produced in a dense cluster at the top of the stem. Indigenous plants have petals that are red with a white base while cultivated varieties have characteristic small flowers with fringed or serrated petals of red, white, pink, purple or a variegated pattern with many cultivars offering a pleasing spicy fragrance. There are both dwarf bedding types as well as taller cut flower varieties with a vase life lasting from 7–10 days. Sweet William prefers a well drained loamy, slightly alkaline soil with sun to partial shade, the flowers be-

ing prolonged with some shading. Propagation is by seed, cuttings or division, however, seeds of cultivars will not breed true. Germination of seeds takes about 5–10 days at 20° C (68° F) with flowering occurring 60–90 days after planting extending from late spring through summer. Deadheading is recommended to encourage further flowering.

Being very floriferous and colourful, the plant is widely used in borders, wall or rock gardens, containers and informal country style gardens. The nectar of Sweet William attracts birds, butterflies and bees, while the edible flowers can add colour to salads, marmalade, fish dishes, sorbet and tea.

Compared to annuals and perennials, the number of biennial species is relatively small, however, whether it is the tall large-flowered Hollyhocks (Althea rosea), the showy, tubular flowers of the Foxglove (Digitalis purpurea) or the short, but bright, attractive and numerous, small rounded inflorescence of Sweet William (Dianthus barbatus), biennials can be most attractive as a component of the flower garden. 🐜

See page 104-105 for photos.

Biennial Vegetables
by Ed Czarnecki

Radish
(Patrickov)

There are a number of cultivated vegetables that are biennial but are grown as root crops storing food in the bulb, root or tuber during the first year and flowering to produce seed in its second year. Examples include the onion (*Allium cepa*), beets (*Beta vulgaris*), radish (*Raphanus sativus*), turnip (*Brassica napus*), salsify or 'vegetable oyster' (*Tragopogon porrifolius*), carrot (*Daucus carota*), parsnip (*Pastinaca sativa*) and turnip-rooted chervil (*Chaerophyllum bulbosum*).

Onion (*Allium cepa*)

Several species of Allium have been used as food since very early times with onion and garlic being consumed in Egypt about 3000 BC. Today, onions and other relatives are used either as separate vegetables or as flavourings with other foods in most parts of the world. Although its origin is uncertain, onions are widely grown and exported in large quantities. In culinary use onions may be eaten raw, fried, roasted and boiled, used in soups, sauces, stews, curries and as a major ingredient in pickles and chutneys.

The bulb is composed of fleshy enlarged leaf-bases and varies in colour from white to red to dark brown while in shape from oval to globose to a flattened globose.

Beets (*Beta vulgaris*)

Beets or "beetroot" which belong to the Goosefoot family (*Chenopodiaceae*) are closely related to the sugar beet, mangolds, spinach beets and chards. They are believed to be derived from the indigenous subspecies *maritima* native to Europe, North Africa, and from Asia Minor to the West Indies. Beets may be used as a salad ingredient, but may also be boiled, peeled and eaten fresh, cooked or cold or pickled in brine. It is also a main ingredient in *Borscht,* a popular soup in Eastern Europe. Due to the high sugar content, beets have also been used in making wine. In horticulture, the beet shape is classified as 'globe', 'long', or 'intermediate'.

Radish (*Raphanus sativus*)

Radishes are thought to have originated in Southern Asia but are of unknown origin or in the wild state. They were grown in Egypt over 2000 years ago and various forms are cultivated world-wide. Radish vary in colour from red, pink, white, purple or black and in shape from round to cylindrical. The roots of radish are generally eaten raw as a vegetable, combined in a salad or cooked in soups. It can also be preserved by pickling.

Turnip (*Brassica rapa* var. *rapa*)

The turnip, which belongs to the *Cruciferacea* family, is a root vegetable grown primarily in temperate climates worldwide for its white, bulbous taproot. It may be eaten cooked in various ways, but the green leafy type (turnip greens) are popular as well, resembling mustard greens in flavour. Smaller, more tender varieties are grown for human consumption, while the larger types are grown as a livestock feed. Speciality varieties, known as "baby turnips", come in white-, yellow-, orange- and red-fleshed varieties. They can be eaten whole, including their leaves and are only available when freshly harvested as they do not keep well. The flavour of baby turnips is mild, so they can be eaten raw in salads.

Salsify (*Tragopogon porrifolius*)

Another name for salsify is the oyster plant (because its roots are supposedly of a similar taste to oysters). Salsify is a native of southern Europe. The white roots are eaten through the winter either boiled, baked or as a creamed soup while the tender young leaves make a palatable salad.

Carrot (*Daucus carota*)

Carrots, which were known to the Greeks and Romans, are now cultivated throughout the world. The carrot is a rich source of vitamin A and its high sugar content is indicative of its sweetness. Not only are carrots valuable for human consumption, but are also useful for livestock feeding. The finely divided leaves are an added ornamental attraction and if left to grow for a second year, the plant bears a terminal compound umbel of white flowers subtended by ternate (growing in threes) or pinnatifed (feather form) bracts.

Parsnip (*Pastinaca sativa*)

Parsnips have been cultivated since Roman times and wild parsnip is locally abundant in England and Wales, but also occurring in much of Europe and the Caucasus. It has been introduced into other parts of the world. The large, tapering, fleshy, edible white root of parsnip has a distinct flavour and is usually served as a cooked vegetable. Wine and beer have been made from parsnip. Near the end of summer the solids of the root consist mainly of starch, but a period of low temperature changes much of the starch to sugar.

The root is hardy and can be left in the ground all winter without deterioration. It is also used as a livestock feed.

Turnip-rooted Chervil (*Chaerophyllum bulbosum*)

This biennial is native to southern Europe and is sometimes cultivated for its roots, which are 10–13 cm (4–5 in) long and grey or blackish in colour with sweet yellow flesh. They are lifted in summer when the foliage dries out and may be stored like potatoes. They are used in stews, or boiled and served as a vegetable dish. 🐾

See page 105 for photos.

Callas and Cannas – The Other Lilies
by Carla Hrycyna

I s it the tropical looking foliage or the unique flower that attracts us to cannas and callas? Both are called lilies but neither are true 'lilies'. Both vary in height and colour and are often used both in garden beds and container plantings. Cannas are commonly seen en masse in commercial plantings. The structure created by using both cannas and callas is dramatic and outstanding.

Canna Lilies

The Canna Lily belongs in the family of Cannacaea, native to the southern states and South America. The canna has rhizomatous rootstock. Large tropical, alternate leaves grow along one central stalk in a graceful unfurling motion. Depending on the variety, the leaves of cannas may be green, green with striations of white banding, reddish burgundy or with variegated green and yellow striping. A flower tops each stalk in colours ranging from yellow, pink, red or orange, depending on the variety. Heights vary from ½–2½ m (2–8 ft) (known as dwarf, semi-dwarf, unique or variegated and tall respectively). They are used widely for patio, deck or garden plantings. When planting canna rhizomes, it is sometimes difficult to know which end is up, so planting the rhizome on its side will ensure the proper growth of the leaf stalk. Cannas, like callas, are

Canna Lily 'Red King Humbert'
(Carla Hrycyna)

best planted early in containers, to be planted in the garden or other decorative containers, at a later frost free time. They prefer to be planted in full sun for optimal blooming. Delayed planting of cannas will result in foliage with little or no bloom. The rhizomes should be lifted in the fall, after the leaves have experienced a few nights of light frost.

Tall varieties:

Canna 'Red King Humbert' tops out at 2 m (6 ft) tall with red flowers and bronze red foliage.

Canna 'Wyoming' ranges from 2–3 m (6–9 ft) depending on the length of the growing season. It is graced with orange bloom on green leaves with a strong bronze edge.

Semi-Dwarf varieties:
Canna 'Miss Oklahoma' possesses medium green leaves with a deep coral and pink bloom reaching 1 m (3 ft) tall.

Canna 'Crimson Beauty Dwarf' has bright emerald green leaves with bright crimson red or pink blooms.

Dwarf:
Canna 'Lucifer' is a true dwarf at ⅔ m (2 ft) tall with bright green foliage banded with a yellow edge and a bright orange-red flower.

Unique & Variegated
Canna 'Futurity' series are re-blooming cannas (a bonus for any gardener) with dark burgundy colour in the leaves, flowers ranging from pink, red, rose and yellow.

Canna 'Pretoria' is probably the most unique with its truly tropical looking foliage of variegated cream, yellow and green striping. Its bright orange bloom is an added bonus to this variety.

Calla Lilies

Calla Lilies (*Zantedeschia*) or arum lily have origins from Africa. They are found mostly in the bulb form, and can also be purchased in plant form during the spring and summer. The bulb is in the form of a tuber with small unusual growths on them. Calla lily tubers have slight fingerling attachments on them. Usually you can see the beginning of the bud formation where new growth will emerge. (Like cannas, if you are unsure as to which end is up, plant the tuber on its side and the plant will correct its growth habit.) Monitor the amount of water used when growing any type of tuber indoors, as too much water will rot a tuber if there is not sufficient air circulation. Bottom heat is important when forcing tubers or bulbs. One tuber may produce multiple stems of leaves, and flowers. The arrowhead shaped leaves of the calla may be bright green, some with a white speckling of colour splashed over the leaves. Like canna lilies, it is best to start callas early indoors for successful blooming. It generally takes 7–9 weeks of growth before blooming occurs. Calla lilies should be grown in full sun to part sun locations, either in containers or in garden settings. The elegant cup-like blooms are often used in wedding bouquets, with white being the most used colour. Blooms are available in a full range of colour – yellow, ivory blush, pink, rose, hot pink, ruby red, and purple to black. Most range in height from 25–60 cm (10–24 in) tall.

Cannas and callas are not hardy to the prairie garden. Both of these may be lifted in the fall after frost has occurred. Lift the bulbs; remove the dried foliage, leaving a 8 cm (3 in) of the stalk attached. Clean, dry rhizomes are best stored in a cool (not freezing), dark environment. Clean sawdust or peat moss may be used to store the rhizomes with a sprinkling of sulphur dust to prevent mold and disease. Each year you will see your canna and calla bulbs multiply.

Both cannas and calla lilies add a blend of exotic tropical flare. Either mass plantings of cannas or the delicate focal point of a calla, will add a strong impact to your garden. My favourite is a mass planting of large cannas in large pots on a deck or poolside for dramatic tropical paradise. 🏵

See page 106 for photos.

Calla and Canna Care Table
by Claire Berube

Spring Care		
	Calla	**Canna**
Stage 1	Use new soil every year. Soil must be sterile or soilless. Plant six to eight weeks before last frost. Plant in a deep container (10–13cm/4–5in deep) or gallon pot. Plant rhizome horizontally with growing side up (eyes up). Keep soil moist until first leaves appear.	Divide rhizome in Spring, keeping only the most healthy roots. Use rich, sterile soil at growing stage. Plant in early March for late June, early July bloom. Plant rhizome horizontally with a minimum of two to three eyes per rhizome. Plant 10–13 cm (4–5 in) deep in gallon pot or bigger. Water generously at planting, then moderately.
Stage 2 (week 3)	Fertilize with a balanced fertilizer, 20-20-20, when first leaves come up and are 5cm/2in high.	Don't over-water, too much water kills plants. Fertilize with a balanced formula (20-20-20).
Stage 3 (weeks 5 to 7)	Watch watering to make sure leaves stay green and do not yellow from too much watering.	Fertilize with four parts blood and bone meal and one part sulphate of potash per gallon pot at week 7 (total amount per gallon pot = 1 tbsp).
Stage 4 (week 8) or when nights are warmer	Place 30cm/12in apart in garden or next to pond to allow room to spread. Plant calla at same depth as in pot. Water plentifully, but do not over water. Feed bi-monthly with half-strength compost tea or with balanced fertilizer at ¾ strength. Overnight temperatures must be above 12° C (54° F).	Plant canna at same depth as in pot. Place 40 cm (16 in) apart in garden. Prefers full sun, preferably rich and moist soil, but not wet. Will tolerate hot, sunny sites. At a minimum, water thoroughly once a week during dry spells. Fertilize once a month with 20-20-20 during active growing. Overnight temperatures must be above 10° C (50° F).

Fall Care		
	Calla	**Canna**
Late summer care	Cut back watering slightly in mid-August until leaves turn light yellow and droop to the ground.	Stop fertilizing in late August.
Best time to lift	Mid- to late-September when temperatures stay in the mid 20°'s C (68° F) range during the day and no lower than 10°C (50° F) overnight. Dig up when leaves lying on the ground. Cut stems back to ground level before lifting.	After 1st light frost -3° C (27° F). (Late September to early November depending on year).
Eyes per rhizome	Minimum of three, but more is usual.	Minimum of three to five. More takes too much room.
Storage	Let rhizome dry for one hour Pack in dry peat moss, horizontally, eyes up. Store in cardboard box in frost-free location at temperature of no less than 8° C (46° F) or higher than 12° C (54° F).	Dig up rhizome carefully and leave a small amount of soil around root. Let dry until soil falls off with a shake of the rhizome. Store upside down in dry peat moss in large boxes or wire/plastic crates in a dry, frost-free location. Temperature should be no less than 5° C (41° F) and no higher than 10° C (50° F).

The Calla Lily symbolizes
the Present and Beauty.

There are biblical and Buddhist references as to how the plants do not worry about the future, and how we should remember that we are loved as much as the plants.

Geraniums
by Ray Mryglod

Greenhouse Assistant (5 years)
St. Mary's Nursery & Garden Centre

Geraniums have long been garden staples throughout Canada. The popular geraniums you find at most garden centres belong to the genus *Pelargonium*. It is difficult to trace the parentage after years of hybridization, but most will fall into six major groups, with zonals subdivided further:

Angels
Angels have dainty little flowers, almost like pansies. The first variety 'Angeline' was listed in the 1820's. The leaves are small, with a plant height of 45–50 cm (18–20 in). They are admired by all who see them and are ideal for bedding, garden tubs and window boxes. Angels

do best in a large tub, urn, or even hanging baskets. Fertilize well, especially during spring. Angels do not like wet feet, and should have fast draining potting mix for best results.

Ivy
This trailing geranium has ivy-like leaves, and is also referred to as a 'Pillar' geranium. Their long, trailing stems make them ideal for hanging baskets, window boxes and containers of all kinds. Their flowers are more subdued than their more flamboyant cousins, more toned to the pastel range of colour. Older varieties are somewhat intolerant of long periods of heat and humidity, but newer varieties are more heat-resistant. The common name springs from the shape of the leaves. The Ivy type can tolerate some shade as well.

Regals
The spectacular large blooms of the Regal Geranium (also known as the Martha Washington Geranium) come in shades of red, purple, pink, and white. Their leaves are stiff and pleated. Flowering occurs in late spring and summer. In most areas of

Geranium leaves
(Kelly MacDonald)

Canada they are treated as an annual because they are intolerant of frost. They require some afternoon shade during the hot summer months and require more water than most geraniums. Because they dislike intense heat and humidity, Regal Geraniums are well suited for northern regions' summers. If you fertilize them weekly, they will bloom all summer. They require care similar to that of Zonals. Regals don't tolerate heat as well, and will cease blooming as a result. The best place for these plants is morning sun and afternoon shade. They bloom in white and vivid colours such as orange, purple, red and burgundy. In some parts of Canada these plants can grow up to 1¼ m (4 ft) tall!

Shrubby Leaved

These shrubby plants are grown primarily for their foliage, and have aromatic leaves of apple, balsam, citrus, rose, and mint, and other scents. The plants have modest flowers and can grow to 1 m (3 ft) tall. Some citrus-scented types such as 'Citrosa' or 'Citronella,' repel mosquitoes.

Unique

These geraniums can withstand the sun better than other pelargonium varieties. They are excellent plants to border a vegetable garden or for the perennial bed, as they will flower throughout the season. Many look like ferns. Uniques require more water than regular zonal pelargoniums.

Zonal

This group is loved for its big, attractive flower heads that bloom white, pink, orange, red or purple. The leaves have a dark zonal pattern on the leaves. If given proper care and sufficient light, zonals will bloom through the whole season. There are so many varieties of zonal, one would be hard-pressed not to find that right one! They are: erect and bushy, Cactus-flowered, Dwarf, Double-flowered, Fancy-leaved, Single flowered, Stellar, Miniatures and Scented leaved.

There you have a brief breakdown of the many types of geranium you can find. Whether you need plants for urns, hanging baskets, borders, displays, in beds or pots, there will be a geranium for you!

Now, how do you look after these beauties? Although they can weather a light frost, geraniums love to bask in warm weather.

Pelargonium
'Happy Thought'

Geranium Requirements

Light
Most types flower best in full sun, (six hours of direct sun a day). Many geraniums will do quite well in part shade, but they won't flower as prolifically. Zonals like the same lower humidity we do, not the humid hothouse conditions of ferns or orchids. They should not be put in saucers of water as the root area will soon rot. If a saucer is used, it should be emptied a few minutes after watering. If given proper care and sufficient light, zonals will bloom most of the year. An excellent rule of thumb to follow is the less green on the leaf (ie. the more brown or red) the less direct sun the plant can tolerate.

Soil
Geraniums like rich soil that is well drained. Compost added to your soil is a welcome added boost.

Fertilizer
Geraniums are heavy feeders. Fertilizer every two weeks with a water-soluble fertilizer such as 20-20-20. Alternatively you may feed them at planting time with a time-release fertilizer that lasts all season. Regular fertilizing is especially important for container-grown plants.

Water
The most important thing to remember about watering geraniums is to water them thoroughly, but let the soil dry between waterings. Check containers daily during hot summer weather. If it's dry two inches down or more, it's time to water.

Grooming
Leaves can die and turn brown for a number of reasons, mostly because geraniums are quite sensitive to fungal disease from excess moisture and humidity. Keep your plants looking their best by deadheading them and removing dried or discoloured leaves. Your geraniums will reward you by looking great all season. 🌱

See page 107 for photos.

The language of flowers was a Victorian-era means of communication in which various flowers were used to send coded messages, allowing individuals to express feelings.

Geranium = Gentility

Seed to Success
by Carla Hrycyna

Imagine a seed, the size of the 'dot' made from a newly sharpened pencil, or some much larger, as large as a bean. Extremely small seeds, such as nicotiana, make seeding difficult even for those with the best dexterity, while marigolds, beans and peas are wonderful for children to try for their first time seeding experience. Seed colour varies from dark shiny black seed, like pansy seed, to the multicoloured pea-like seeds of lupines. Shape is interesting as well: rounded like petunia, straight tubular like marigold, or flattened arrowhead-like shape of zinnia. Regardless of seed size or shape, there are steps to successful seeding.

The whole process of seeding begins with the seed. The germination rate of new 'fresh' seed is higher than that of seed which has been sitting around the garden shed for too many seasons. Seed packets will sometimes list the germination rate of the seed contained within a package. Seeding schedules are an important part in knowing the when, where and how's of seeding.

Each seed germinates and begins its life cycle in a time frame. This guides the gardener to sow seeds, allowing time for germination, growth and production of flower or fruit.

Seed is either sown directly in the garden or can be started indoors for an earlier blooming time. The purpose of this article is to assist you in seeding plants indoors for earlier planting in the garden.

Tips
- Use a light peat based starter mix for seeding. A lighter seed mix allows for proper seed emergence.
- Keep growing medium uniformly moist to ensure germination.
- Do not choose overly large containers when first seeding. It is better to use smaller cell containers and then transplant to a larger unit as the plant and root develops.
- Seed planting depth depends on the size of the seeds. Generally, smaller seeds (petunia, pansy,

Sunflower seedlings

nicotiana) are planted at the surface with a small dusting of soil on top. Larger seeds are generally planted at a depth of four times the seed width, as with lupines, sweet peas, and nasturtiums.

- Keep a 'dome' cover of clear plastic over the seed trays to create a humid environment.
- It is recommended to place your seed trays in a warm location (such as the top of the fridge) or on a heating pad. Seeds germinate at different rates – i.e. marigolds at two–four days, petunias at seven days, datura at 14-21 days. This is due to the 'embryo' coating of the seed. Some coatings are harder than others. Marigolds, for example, are very softly coated and germinate very quickly. Pansy seed, being slightly harder, require more moisture, heat and humidity to help break the outer seed coating. Lupines have very hard outer coatings that require longer periods of humidity, heat and oxygen to enable germination. Seeds with harder seed coatings are often recommended to have a pre-soak period to help soften the outer shell of the seed. Other methods of ensuring seed germination are scarification: nicking or scarring thicker seeds like morning glories with a sharp knife or rubbing sand paper on the seeds assists the harder seed to 'break'. Pre-chilling your seeds will help too. Seeds dropped by plants in the fall go through a natural

'chilling' period; poppies and other perennial seeds benefit from this process. I have seeded for 14 years on a commercial basis, and always pre-chill our seeds.

- Always check the 'days to germination' on the seed package. Seeds with similar germination periods can be seeded together in the same tray. Leggy or 'stretched' plants may result if seeded with others of varying germination times.
- Lighting is a factor with most seeds, though some seeds prefer darkness to germinate (i.e. pansies, violas, verbena and delphiniums).

As soon as you see the emergence of the hypocotyls (first root), remove the covered dome to prevent the seedling from 'stretching'.

Soon you will see the emergence of the cotyledon leaves (not the 'true leaves'). This is the point where plants will either thrive or experience a 'damping off' (show signs of wilting, sometimes looking like they have been 'pinched' on their stem, causing the new seedling to fall over). This is the stage where careful watering should occur.

Early seeding is like candy to a kid (at least I think it is). We plan, plant and care for the tiniest of seeds, waiting in anticipation of the first leaf, thinking of all the loveliest of blooms that will follow. If you have never seeded an annual, biennial or perennial before, I invite you to try. It is fun, relaxing and rewarding! ❧

Designing Flowerbeds with Annuals and Creating an English Cottage Garden in the Prairies

by Rosie Chard

Rosie Chard BSc. LI Dip. Part III ((London) MLA (MALA). Landscape Design Office with St. Mary's Nursery and author of novel 'Seal Intestine Raincoat'

The English cottage garden had a humble beginning. Originating in England during the sixteenth century, the first examples consisted of small plots of land adjacent to peasants' cottages. These areas functioned initially as kitchen gardens, providing much needed space for vegetables, small livestock and beehives. Any leftover soil was filled with flowers. As interest in garden design grew amongst the wealthier landowners, the formal gardens of previous eras began to be replaced by informal garden spaces that recognized the aesthetic qualities of the cottage garden: informality, simple charm and an abundance of flowers.

Cottage gardening as a pastime evolved over the ensuing centuries, which grew in popularity during the Victorian era with the writings of William Robinson and Gertrude Jekyll, before culminating in the large-scale, early twentieth century masterpieces at Sissinghurst and Hidcote in southern England.

The contemporary English cottage garden has special qualities. Its intimate nature appeals to the senses with its use of scent, subtle combinations of colour and dense textured planting. It is also nostalgic, jogging our memories about real or imagined outdoor pleasures. These essential qualities can be recreated in the Prairies using a mixture of annuals and hardy perennials. There is a wealth of native and ornamental flowers available here that will flourish in our climate and can be used to create a romantic and informal atmosphere.

Sissinghurst Castle Gardens

For the purist, a true cottage garden has no lawn, possesses a well-defined sense of enclosure, usually hedges, and is filled with a wide range of flowers. This is a higher maintenance form of gardening than one with lawns, but it does not always have to be labour intensive. The cottage garden can vary in size. It can be adapted to the individual site either filling the whole yard, forming part of a larger yard, or growing within a strategically placed smaller bed.

Although there is the appearance of informality, the well-executed English cottage garden follows all the design principles of other forms of outdoor space: composition, harmony, balance, proportion, rhythm, repetition and colour. The relationship of the garden to the 'cottage' or home is crucial and use is made of other design elements such as focal points and vistas.

The key to successful planting design is contrast. When plants of similar size and shape are grouped together, the effect can be bland and uninspiring. Only by juxtaposing plants with contrasting characteristics, do the unique qualities of each become apparent. This contrast applies to all aspects of the plant, including colour, overall plant form, flower, bud and seed head shape, leaf shape and texture, transparency and solidity.

Choice of colour has a significant effect on the atmosphere of the garden. A single colour border has an elegant simplicity to it that accentuates contrasts in other characteristics of the plants such as leaf or flower shape. Choosing a limited palette of colours creates a relaxing, harmonious effect. The traditional English flower garden evolved in the temperate climate of northern Europe beneath grey skies and low levels of light, so the classic colours used were mainly soft hues of pink, pale blue, lilac and white with small amounts of purple. The dazzling blue skies and intense light levels of Western Canada allow the effective use of brighter colours in the border, where the rich yellow of nasturtium and the blood red of poppies can be utilized to give a more intense colour combination. The use of complimentary colours in plant groupings is another way of harmonizing the border. The deep purple of petunias coupled with the lemon yellow of violas gives a lovely effect, while planting orange dahlias next to blue lobelias brings out the depth of colour in each of them.

In the absence of structure forming shrubs the larger, more structural annuals take on a greater role in giving the borders height and depth. Hollyhocks, *Malva*, Larkspur and the taller Rudbeckias all serve this purpose while at the same time contributing colour and scent. By contrasting different plant forms the border becomes more interesting. The vertical accent of foxgloves and larkspur contrast well with the more rounded forms of plants such as cosmos.

The same principal applies to individual flower shapes. Cleomes look like spiders, Centurea have buttons, stock flowers are butterflies while members of the Salvia family all have distinct spikes. These shapes can be assembled in various ways to form a secondary layer of contrast. Flower buds also make their contribution. The miniature buds of baby's breath add a lightness to the flowerbed while the buds of Centurea, with its finely textured patterning, resemble tiny, delicate artichokes. Seed heads can be used to provide interest later in the season. Love-in-the-mist and honesty both produce copious amounts of seeds encased inside intriguingly shaped pods while the seed heads of poppies, nasturtium, and scabiosa are all striking in unique ways.

Although the cottage garden is mainly about flowers, the use of varying leaf shapes and textures heightens their effect. The light filigree of cosmos leaves contrasts well with the boldness of Nasturtium; and the deeply veined foliage of Heliotrope looks good beside the ferny foliage of the Dahlberg daisy.

The amount of transparency and solidity in a garden bed is also worth considering. Some flowers are naturally transparent; the tissue-like petals of poppies contrast well with the solid flowers of Gazania while some plants are naturally 'see-through' in form, such as *Verbena bonariensis*, which, although tall, can be planted in drifts in front of smaller plants to give the bed a sense of mystery.

Fragrance is an essential part of the cottage garden and there are many flowers growing in the Prairies that are known for their scents. Lavender is one of the quintessential aromas of the English cottage garden and there are few things more enjoyable than smelling the sherbet aroma of Heliotrope or the rich scent of purple petunias. Plants produce fragrance at different times of the day. Stocks and tobacco flowers release their intoxicating scents during the evening, while sweet peas and alyssum are just two examples of flowers that perfume the daytime air.

It is important not to forget the dynamic and tactile qualities of a garden. Choosing plants that respond to a breeze can give the border a lightness and sense of movement that animates the whole yard. Grasses are particularly sensitive to subtle changes in air movement and the leaves and feathery flowers of fountain grass are particularly lovely on a windy day. For anyone who has ever planted it, there is nothing more beautiful than the lilac clusters of *Verbena bonarien-*

Variety in shape and texture
(Carla Hrycyna)

sis swaying in the wind in the middle of a large flower garden. Wildlife can also add to movement in a garden. Many flowers attract bees and butterflies and it is fascinating to see these creatures darting from flower to flower as they gather nectar.

As well as admiring and smelling flowers, it is fun to touch them. Annual grasses such as *Stipa* are soft to the touch while the comical flowers of snapdragons and catapulting seeds of balsam have been enchanting children since they first arrived in the Prairies.

Annuals need not be confined to the garden. Many flowers can be cut and enjoyed inside the house. Snapdragons and carnations easily retain their shape in a vase of water while statice and salvias take particularly well to being dried and used in flower arrangements.

Certain things must be borne in mind when planning and planting a cottage garden, as it has a short and intense life. Annuals should not be planted out before the third week in May. Attention must be given to fertilizing, watering, weeding and deadheading, but as the plants grow and cover more soil, the amount of weeding will diminish. The cottage garden is traditionally quite densely planted with tall plants at the back, medium plants in the centre and small plants at the front of the bed. Plants look best when planted in groups of at least three and odd numbers look more natural than even. This sense of naturalness is also enhanced by

the positioning of the plant material. Interlocking drifts of flowers are preferable to concise blocks.

One of the pleasures of the cottage garden is that it can change from year to year. Flowers will seed themselves in surprising places, nasturtium may crawl onto a path, poppies may turn up unexpectedly in a forgotten corner of limestone gravel and the owner can easily make minor adjustments.

Annuals can be mixed with other plants: trees, shrubs and perennials, to create a more permanent bed. They can also be used to temporarily fill any seasonal gaps in the border, either planted directly into the soil or slipped between other plants while still in a pot. Vegetables and herbs may also be incorporated into the beds. Leeks have attractive white ball-shaped flowers, while rosemary adds an unforgettable scent.

Although it may appear natural and unstructured, creating an English cottage garden takes planning. But spending the cold winter evenings thumbing through seed and annual catalogues is a pleasure in itself. With a short, yet intense growing season, the Prairies are particularly suited to the growing of annuals, and with careful planning and regular maintenance, there is no reason why a yard with all the qualities of an English cottage garden cannot be created here. 🪶

See page 108 for photos.

Osteos
by Ray Myrglod

Osteospermum are delightful plants originating from South Africa. Their name is derived from the Greek osteon(bone) and Latin spermum (seed). Osteospermums belong to the daisy family and are also known as the African Daisy or South African Daisy, Cape Daisy and Blue-Eyed Daisy. They are an annual plant in regions colder than Zone 9.

Osteospermums are relatively new to most gardeners, but have steadily risen in popularity in the last decade as they have become more commercially available. With a mature height of 15–25 cm (6–10 in), these plants are excellent choices as summer bedding plants for pots or in borders, beds or window boxes.

The 5 cm (2 in) flower heads have a central disc and petals in the shape of ray florets. They come in several colours, including white, cream, pink, purple, mauve to yellow. Newer varieties may have a different shade at the tips, or towards the end of the petal. One of my favourites is the purple spoon shaped petal type called Whirlygig.

Osteospermums must be planted in a sunny position in well drained soil. If you have heavy clay, like we do here in Winnipeg, drainage can easily be improved by adding substrate, peat, grit or compost. Don't allow the plants to dry out completely, especially in the first two weeks after planting when the roots are trying to establish themselves.

Osteospermums require cooler nights for production of the flower buds. If the night temperatures remain high, they will stop flowering for a period. The petals of most Osteospermums close in the evenings, although there are now a few new varieties that stay open longer at night.

Watering: Osteos are prone to drying out in the full sun, particularly when in pots. It is essential to water regularly. If they dry out, the plants will go into 'sleep mode' and will not easily come back into flower. Additionally, if roots are apt to rot if watered after drying out. The rule of thumb is 'evenly moist'.

Feeding: For best results feed your Osteospermums on a weekly basis with a general fertilizer such as Phostrogen. This will help promote flowering.

Dead Heading: Remove wilted flowers on a regular basis to prolong new flowers. To prevent a straggly appearance, take off part of the flower stem to tidy up the plant.

Enjoying: Osteospermums pair wonderfully with the delicate fragrant alyssum along borders, or in pots with lobelia. I had much success last summer with long window boxes full of varied osteos, lobelia and hanging bacopa. I give these lovely robust plants two thumbs up!

The Sun's Flower
by Evelyn Ione Turner

Evelyn has her Diploma in Horticulture, University of Guelph 2009

Helianthus annuus (common sunflower) is a perfect example of the many showstoppers that belong to the *Asteraceae* family. What we recognize and often consider to be one flower is actually countless disc florets (also known as our beloved sunflower seeds), which are surrounded by numerous ray florets (our showy coloured petals).

Sunflowers are easy to seed. They germinate rapidly and have a high germination rate which makes them appealing to the novice, the experimental gardener and the less patient. Although a sunflower can be grown in well drained soil and adores a full day's sun, it will also grow with as little as 6 hours of sunlight.

Sunflowers can be found in all heights, sizes, colours, with and without pollen, and stake or stake-free varieties. This plant can have single or double blooms (Teddy Bear ⅔–1 m/2–3 ft). The colour possibilities are endless with various shades of yellows to bi-coloured (Ring Of Fire 1¼–1½ m/4–5 ft) to multicoloured reds (Chianti 1¼–1½ m/4–5 ft) to almost white (Italian white 1¼–1½ m/4–5 ft).

From borders to backdrops, *Helianthus annuus* has many homes in our gardens and containers. Big Smile (30–38 cm/12–15 in) and Pacino (30–40 cm/12–16 in) are just the right single dwarfed varieties for that 'simply fun' border or edge in a landscaped space. From the ideal cut flower pollen-less Soraya (1½–1¾m/5–6 ft) to the huge Giganteus (3–4 m/10–13 ft), there are countless varieties to accommodate one's gardening desires.

The sunflower is also a wonderful example of heliotropism (a plant that follows the sun). This face that mimics the sun's east to west movement throughout the day is both an ornamental beauty in our gardens and containers, and an essential crop of our prairie lands. Sunflower seeds have many uses; they can be roasted and salted for our favourite snack foods, processed for the highest quality cooking oils, used to feed a family hamster or our sociable wild birds.

The sun's flowers are perfect for our prairie gardens. They are friendly to the blackest thumbs, to the gardening youngsters or to the veterans of our gardening world. 🐦

The 2010 Prairie Garden Colour Section

A mixed container of coleus, geraniums
& lobelia, that won an award in the 2007
East Kildonan Garden Club (Winnipeg,
MB) competition.
(Stefan Fediuk)

Gaura lindheimeri 'Belleza'
(Jim Kohut)

Artemisia 'Oriental Limelight'
(Jim Kohut)

Using Perennials As Annuals
see page 3

Beebalm
(Victor Dyck)

Rudbeckia hirta 'Prairie Sun'
(Jim Kohut)

Vinca minor 'Illumination'
(Jim Kohut)

Uninvited Annuals
see page 19

Johnny Jump-Up
(Victor Dyck)

**Self Seeding Feverfew
and Sweet Rocket**
(Fran Wershler)

Impatiens
see page 22

Fiesta Burgandy
(Carla Hrycyna)

Super Elfin Pearl Blue
(Carla Hrycyna)

Double Impatiens
(Valerie Denesiuk)

Rudbeckia
'Autumn Charm'
(Carla Hrycyna)

Kale
(Valerie Denesiuk)

Falling for Flowers (the Cool Ones!)
see page 23

Viola hybrid
(Valerie Denesiuk)

Page 93

Marigolds
see page 27

French Vanlla
(Carla Hrycyna

Durango Bolero
(Carla Hrycyna

Osteospermum 101
see page 43

Serenity White Bliss
(Jared Van Beveren)

Summertime Purple Spoon
(Jared Van Beveren)

Summertime Sunshine
(Jared Van Beveren)

Understanding Coleus:
the Garden's Kaleidoscope
see page 33
(all photos Dr. Bob Bors)

'Kiwi Fern'   'Night Time'

'Sundown'   'Sunrise'

Results of students experimenting with breeding coleus in winter to produce an alternative crop to poinsettias.

Understanding Coleus:
the Garden's Kaleidoscope

see page 33

(all photos Bob Bors)

'Pineapple' and
'Texas Parkinglot'

'Saturn'

A 'Christmas-type coleus',
under development

Orange Coleus: some coleus varieties are
more subject to fading of older leaves

Petunias

see page 31

Ultra Crimson Star
(Valerie Denesiuk)

Supertunia Lavender Skies
(Proven Winners)

Sweetunia Extreme Yello
(Carla Hrycyna)

Potunia Lobster
(Jared Van Bevern)

An older 'Pendula' type
(Sylvia Wilson)

The Nonstop Begonia

An Exotic for Prairie Gardens

see page 38

Nonstop Begonia Mocca Orange
(Carla Hrycyna)

'Fire' a recent introduction
(Sylvia Wilson)

A Nonstop grouping
(Sylvia Wilson)

Dahlias for the Prairies
see page 45

Collarette Form
(John Rempel)

Formal Decorative Form
(John Rempel)

Informal Decorative Form
(John Rempel)

Ball Form Dahlia "Jessie G"
(John Rempel)

Formal Decorative Form
(Valerie Denesiuk)

Incurved Cactus Form
(Valerie Denesiuk)

Fuschia

see page 48

Fuschia bloom
close-up
(Frank Kovalchek)

Fuschia
(Valerie Denesiuk)

Ipomea Sweet Caroline Series
(Carla Hrycyna)

Solanum laxum
(Wildfeuer)

The Other Potato Plants –
Ipomoeas and Solanums
see page 50

Page 100

Hollyhock
(Wouter Hagens)

Common Mallow
(Alvesgaspa)

The Ukrainian
Malva
see page 52

Gladiolus 'Priscilla'
(Pharaoh Hound)

Growing Gladiolus
see page 137

Gladiolus specie
(Valerie Denesiuk)

Dianthus
(Carla Hrycyna)

Snapdragon 'Liberty Red'
(Carla Hrycyna)

Cool
Annuals
see page 55

Pansy 'Matrix Yellow'
(Carla Hrycyna)

Godetia
(Valerie Denesiuk)

Carnation
(Yakovlev Sergey)

Viola Blueberry Cream
(Carla Hrycyna)

Grandpa Ott
Morning glory
(Valerie Denesiuk)

Lotus vine
(Valerie Denesiuk)

Mandevilla vine
(Valerie Denesiuk)

Annual Vines
see page 56

The edible Malabar
Spinach Vine
(Valerie Denesiuk)

Swayed to Use Grasses
see page 62

'Karl Foerster' Feather Grass
(Jim Kohut)

Fountain Grass
(Valerie Denesiuk)

Viola
(Victor Dyck)

Wishbone flower or Blue wings
(Ken Pei)

Forget-me-not
(Sannse)

Annuals for Shade
see page 65

Biennials
see page 67

Hollyhock
(Marc Ryckaert)

Foxglove
(Foolip)

White Forget-Me-Not
(Thomas G. Barnes)

Sweet William
(Valerie Denesiuk)

Biennials
see page 67

Evening Primrose
(Danny Steaven)

Money Plant flowers
(Teun Spaans)

Money Plant seeds
(Christian Fischer)

Swiss Chard
(Carla Hrycyna)

Allium species
(Wouter Hagens)

Biennial Vegetables
see page 72

Callas and Cannas – The Other Lilies

see page 74

White Calla Lily
(Sandy Venton)

Canna Lily
(Valerie Denesiuk)

Canna Lily
(Valerie Denesiuk)

Geraniums
see page 78

Page 107

'Centennial'
(Carla Hrycyna)

'Apple Blossom Rosebud'
(Valerie Denesiuk)

Martha Washington
'Imperial'
(Valerie Denesiuk)

Designing Flowerbeds with Annuals and Creating an English Cottage Garden in the Prairies
see page 83

(Valerie Denesiuk)

(Valerie Denesiuk)

(Valerie Denesiuk)

Pond Plants
see page 151

(Valerie Denesiuk)

Insects Which Feed on Annual Plants in the Prairie Garden
see page 129

A black swallowtail caterpillar
(Pat Mackay)

Winged morphs of a red aphid
on false sunflower
(Pat Mackay)

Companion Planting
see page 135

Pennyroyal
(Daniel Feliciano)

Ladybug
(Zsolt Barna)

Lupine
(Valerie Denesiuk)

Popular Poppies
see page 142

California Poppy
(Frances Wershler)

Oriental Poppy - Patty's Plum
(Frances Wershler)

Shirley Poppy
(Victor Dyck)

Prince of Orange
(Victor Dyck)

Queen Alexander Oriental Poppy
(Frances Wershler)

Prolific self-seeding California Poppy
(Victor Dyck)

Musings of a
Zone 1 Gardener
see page 157

Lisianthus
(Derek Ramsey)

Himalayan Blue Poppy
(Flowers With Care)

Problems and Solutions for Pine and
Cedar Trees and Shrubs on The Prairies
see page 160

Cedar leaf miner
(Mike Allen)

Cedar scale showing large nymphs
(Mike Allen)

Scale damage
to left cedar
(Mike Allen)

Hellebores
see page 163

Hellebore in early bloom
(Valerie Denesiuk)

Hellebore in late bloom
(Valerie Denesiuk)

To Demystify the Alpine
see page 171

English Cowslip
(Amanda Botincan)

***Orostachys* species**
(Amanda Botincan)

Recommended list of Annuals for the Prairies
see page 121

Double Wax Begonia
(Proven Winners)

Sweet William
(Valerie Denesiuk)

Cosmos
(Fran Wershler)

Cleome 'Violet Queen'
(Carla Hrycyna)

Celosia plumosa 'Castle Mix'
(Carla Hrycyna)

Love-in-a-Mist
(Queerbubbles)

Recommended list of Annuals for the Prairies
see page 121

Strawflower
(Kajetan Dzieranowski)

Lobelia
(Carla Hrycyna)

Snapdragons and a few Petunias
(Fran Wershler)

Datura Purple Ballerina
(Valerie Denesiuk)

Nemesia 'Sunsatia Banana'
(Stan Shebs)

Portulaca 'Sundial Fuschia'
(Carla Hrycyna)

Sweet Pea
(Friedo Stellfeldt)

Page 115

Heliotrope 'Marine'
(Carla Hrycyna)

Salvia Flare
(Carla Hrycyna)

Verbena Bright Eye
(Valerie Denesiuk)

Yellow squash (*Cucurbita*)
(David Monniaux)

Recommended list of Annuals for the Prairies
see page 121

Rudbeckia 'Cherry Brandy'
(Carla Hrycyna)

Salpiglossis
(Valerie Denesiuk)

Sunflower
(Valerie Denesiuk)

Zinnia 'Candy Stripe'
(Valerie Denesiuk)

Pincushion Flower (*Scabiosa*)
(Valerie Denesiuk)

Containers

(Valerie Denesiuk)

(Valerie Denesiuk)

Mix of Coleus & *Lamium*
(Valerie Denesiuk)

Page 118

Containers

Wave Petunia
(Fran Wershler)

(Teresa Lopata)

Wheel barrow
annual container
(Teresa Lopata)

(Valerie Denesiuk)

(Valerie Denesiuk)

Beds of Annuals

Rudbeckia & Coleus
(Carla Hrycyna)

Snapdragons, & Marigolds
(Carla Hrycyna)

Coleus &
Geraniums
(Valerie Denesiuk)

Celosia, Marigolds & Salvia
(Valerie Denesiuk)

Petunias &
Rudbeckia
(Valerie Denesiuk)

'Beauty Shots'

Lantana
(Joaquim Alves Gaspar)

Gaillardia
(Chris Graham)

Gazania
(Noodle Snacks)

Great Masterwort (*Astrantia major*)
(Carla Hrycyna)

Allysum Snow Crystals
(Chris Graham)

Venidium fastuosum 'Zulu Prince'
(Valerie Denesiuk)

Recommended List of Annual Flowers for Manitoba

originally by Manitoba Agriculture, 1979
and revised by Carla Hrycyna and Ed Czarnecki in 2009

The following table of Annual Flowers (or perennial treated as annuals on the prairies) has been found satisfactory for prairie gardens. Some must be sown indoors and transplanted in June, others can be sown outside usually about May 10th where the plants are intended to bloom. For sowing indoors the use of sterilized soil and treating the seed with No-Damp will greatly lessen the chances of 'damping off'. A night temperature of not less than 18°C (65° F), would be satisfactory.

+ Indicates annuals most suitable for bedding
* Most suitable for cutting

Common Name	Botanical Name	Seeding Dates I.=Indoors O.=Outdoors	Height Ft	cm	Colour
African Daisy (blue eyed)	*Arctotis*	I. April 5–20	1	30	Mixed only
Ageratum + (floss flower)	*Ageratum*	I. March 20	½-1	15-30	Blue, pink, white, purple
Alyssum +	*Lobularia*	I. or O. May 10	½	15	White, purple, pink
Amaranthus (Love-lies-bleeding)	*Amaranthus*	O. May 10	2-6	60-180	Mixed foliage colours
Anchusa	*Anchusa*	I. April 1	1½	45	Blue
Angels-trumpet	*Datura Stramonium*	I. March 15	3-5	90-150	White
Asters*+	*Callistephus*	I. March 31 - April 7	1-3	30-90	Various solid colours
Babysbreath *	*Gypsophila*	O. May 1-15	1½	45	White
Bachelor Button	*Centaurea*	I. or O. April 30-May 15	2	60	White, pink, blue, red
Balsam	*Impatiens balsamina*	I. April 15-20	1-3	30-90	Various solid colours
Basil (Dark Opal)	*Ocimum*	I. April 15	1½	45	Purple foliage

Common Name	Botanical Name	Seeding Dates I.=Indoors O.=Outdoors	Height Ft	cm	Colour
Begonia+	Begonia semperflorens	I. February 1	½-1½	15-45	Various solid colours
Bells of Ireland*	Moluccella	I. or O. March 20-31 or late fall	2	60	Green
Blackeyed Susan Vine	Thunbergia	I. March 15	3	90	Orange (trailer)
Blue lace flower	Trachymene	I. or O. May 20-31	1-2	30-60	Blue
Butterfly flower	Schizanthus	I. or O. April 15-30	1½	45	Various solid colours
Calendula + (pot marigold)	Calendula	I. or O. April 15-30	1½	45	Yellow, orange shades
Calliopsis (tickseed)	Coreopsis	I. or O. May 1-15	1-2	30-60	Yellow, red
Candytuft	Iberis	O. April 30	1	30	White, pink, purple, red
Cape Marigold	Dimorphotheca	I. April 15-20	1	30	Mixed only
Carnation*	Dianthus caryophyllus	I. March 15	1-1½	30-45	Various solid colours
Castor Oil Plant	Ricinus	I. Mar. 20-31	5-8	150-240	Red or green foliage
Celosia (plumed) +	Celosia plumosa	O. or I. April 20-30	1-3	30-90	Yellow, red shades
Celosia (cockscomb) +	Celosia cristata	I. April 20-30	1	30	Red, yellow
Chrysanthemum (annual)	Chrysanthemum	I. April 1-15	2	60	Various solid colours
Clarkia	Clarkia	O. May 1-15	2	60	White, pink, red
Chinese Forget-me-not	Cynoglossum	O. April 15-30	1½	45	Blue
Coleus	Coleus	I. March 15	1-2	30-60	Mixed foliage colours
Coneflower	Rudbeckia	I. March 1-15	1½-3	45-90	Yellow, bronze

Common Name	Botanical Name	Seeding Dates I.=Indoors O.=Outdoors	Height Ft	cm	Colour
Cosmos	Cosmos	O. April 15-31	2-5	60-150	Various solid colours
Cup flower	Nierembergia	I. Feb. 20 - March 20	½	15	Blue, purple
Dahlia+	Dahlia	I. Mar. 15-31	2-3	60-90	Various solid colours
Dianthus (Pinks)+	Dianthus	I. Mar. 20-31	1	30	Various solid colours
Meadow Sage	Salvia pratensis	June-Aug.	1½-2	45-60	Blue
Dusty Miller	Cineraria	I. Mar. 15-25	1-2	30-60	Gray foliage
Forget-me-not	Myosotis	I. March 25	1	30	Blue
Four-O'Clock	Mirabilis	O. April 15-25	3	90	Various solid colours
Foxglove (foxy)	Digitalis	I. February 15	2-3	60-90	Pink, mauve
Geranium (seed)	Pelargonium (carefree type, Sprinter)	I. February 1	1½	45	Various solid colours
Globe Amaranth	Gomphrena globosa	I. March 15	1½	45	Reddish purple
Gloriosa Daisy +	Rudbeckia	I. March 1-15	3	90	Yellow, brown
Heliotrope	Heliotropium	I. March 15	1-2	30-60	Blue, purple, white
Horned Viola (Johnny Jump-Up)	Viola cornuta	I. Feb. 20-28	½	15	Various solid colours
Impatiens +	Impatiens	I. March 1	½-3	15-90	Various solid colours
Larkspur	Delphinium ambiguum	O. May 15	3	90	Various solid colours
Larkspur (Chinese)	Delphinium chinensis	I. March 15	1½-2	45-60	Blue, white
Mallow	Lavatera	O. April 15-30	3	90	Pink, red

Common Name	Botanical Name	Seeding Dates I.=Indoors O.=Outdoors	Height Ft	cm	Colour
Livingstone Daisy (Ice Plant)	Dorotheanthus bellidiformis	I. April 15	½	15	Various solid colours
Love-in-a-Mist	Nigella	O. May 1	1½	45	Blue, white
Lobelia	Lobelia erinus	I. March 1-15	½	15	Blue, white, pink
Marigold Tall * +	Tagetes	I. April 15	2-4	60-120	Yellow shades, orange
Marigold Medium +	Tagetes	I. April 15, O. May 5	1-1½	30-45	Yellow shades, orange
Marigold Dwarf +	Tagetes	I. April 15, O. May 5	½-1	15-30	Yellow, red, orange
Mignonette	Reseda	O. May 1-15	1	30	Grown for scent
Morning Glory (dwarf)	Convolvulus	I. or O. April 30	1	30	Blue, mixed
Nasturtium	Tropaeolum	O. May 15	1	30	Yellow, scarlet, orange
Nemesia	Nemesia	I. March 20 - April 7	1	30	Various solid colours
Nicotine	Nicotiana	I. April 15	1½-3	45-90	Various solid colours
Night Scented Stock	Matthiola	O. May 10	1	30	Grown for scent
Pansy +	Viola	I. Feb. 20-28	1	30	Various solid colours
Periwinkle	Vinca rosea	I. March 1-15		15	White, pink, red
Petunia+	Petunia	I. March 31	1	30	Various solid colours
Phlox+	Phlox drummondii	I. April 1-15	½-1	15-30	Various solid colours
Poppy, California	Eschscholtzia californica	O. May 10	1	30	Various solid colours
Poppy, Iceland	Papaver nudicaule	O. April 1-15	2	60	Various solid colours

Common Name	Botanical Name	Seeding Dates I.=Indoors O.=Outdoors	Height Ft	cm	Colour
Poppy, Shirley	*Papaver Rhoeas*	O. May 10	2	60	Various solid colours
Portulaca +	*Portulaca*	I. April 1, O. May 10	½	15	Various solid colours
Queen Anne's Lace (wild carrot)	*Daucus carota*	I. or O. April 15 - May 15	2-3	60-90	White
Salpiglossis	*Salpiglossis*	I. or O. March 15 - April 15	2-3	60-90	Mixed only
Salvia+	*Salvia splendens*	I. March 1-7	¾ -3	20-90	Scarlet, pink, white, purple
Salvia (Mealycup Sage)	*Salvia farinacea*	I. March 1-7	2½-3	75-90	Blue, white
Satin Flower	*Godetia*	O. May 1-15	2	60	Various solid colours
Scarlet Flax	*Linum grandiflorum*	O. April 15	1-1½	30-45	Scarlet
Scabiosa	*Scabiosa*	I. Mar. 15-31	2	60	Various solid colours
Snapdragon +	*Antirrhinum*	I. March 7-15	½ -3	15-90	Various solid colours
Snow-on-the-mountain	*Euphorbia marginata*	O. April 15	1 ½-2	45-60	White-edged foliage
Spider Flower+	*Cleome*	I. Mar. 15-25	3-5	90-150	Pink, white, purple
Statice* (Everlasting)	*Limonium suworowii* or *sinuata*	I. Mar. 20-31	2	60	Various solid colours
Stock*	*Matthiola*	I. April 1-15	1½	45	Various solid colours
Strawflower * (Everlasting)	*Helichrysum*	I. April 15-30	2½	75	Various solid colours
Sunflower *	*Helianthus annus*	O. April 15-30	3-6	90-180	Yellow shades
Sweet William (annual)	*Dianthus barbatus*	I. March 1-15	½-1	15-30	Various solid colours

Common Name	Botanical Name	Seeding Dates I.=Indoors O.=Outdoors	Height Ft	cm	Colour
Sweet Peas *	Lathyrus odoratus	O. May 1-15	1-6	30-180	Various solid colours
Verbena+	Verbena	I. Mar. 20-31	1	45	Various solid colours
Zinnia, Dwarf * +	Zinnia	I. April 20, O. May 15	1-1½	30-45	Various solid colours
Zinnia, giant *+	Zinnia	I. April 20, O. May 15	1½-3	45-90	Various solid colours
Zinnia, Creeping	Sanvitalia	I. April 20, O. May 15	½	15	Orange, brown
Vines					
Morning Glory	Ipomoea	I. or O. April 7-30	10	300	Various solid colours
Cobaea	Cobaea scandens	I. March 25 - April 7	10	300	White, purple
Scarlet Runner Bean	Phaseolus coccineus	O. May 15	10	300	Scarlet
Canary Bird Vine	Tropaeolum	O. May 15	10	300	Yellow
Gourds	Cucurbita	O. May 15	6	180	Colourful fruits

Bedding Plants Other Than Seeded

Cuttings: Marguerite (I. April 1), Geranium, (I. Feb. 1)
Tubers: Madeira vine (I. April 1), Canna (I. Mar. 15), Dahlia (I. April 20, O. May-June), Begonia (I. April 1, O. June 1), Oxalis (O. May 1), Calla lily (O. May 1)
Corms: Gladiolus (O. May 15) 🐌

See page 113-116 for photos.

The language of flowers was a Victorian-era means of communication in which various flowers were used to send coded messages, allowing individuals to express feelings.

Carnation:

Pink = A Woman's Love; White = Disdain;
Purple = Capriciousness, Whimsical, Changeable;
Red = My heart Aches for You; Yellow = You have
Disappointed Me, Rejection, Disdain; Striped = Refusal

Recommended List of Cut Flowers
by Carla Hrycyna and Ed Czarnecki

'Cut Flowers' are plants with blossoms suitable to be cut and displayed in an ornamental vase or other open container of water for aesthetic purposes. This table represents those plants recommended for prairie gardens.

Common Name	Botanical Name	Height		Colour
		cm	ft	
Ageratum (Floss Flower)	Ageratum houstonianum	35–75	1–2½	Blue
Bishops Weed	Ammi majus	60–120	2–4	White, Light Green
Aster	Callistephus chinensis	30–90	1–3	Various Colours
Bells of Ireland	Moluccella laevis	38–50	1–2	Lime–green
Blue Lace Flower	Trachymene coerulea [syn. Didiscus coerulea]	50	2	Sky Blue
Safflower	Carthamus	60–90	2–3	Orange
Celosia Cockscomb	Celosia cristata	90–120	3–4	Various Colours
Celosia Feather	Celosia plumosa	30–60	1–2	Red, Yellow, Pink. Mix
Cosmos	Cosmos bipinnatus	120	4	Various Colours
Dianthus	Dianthus barbatus	30–90	1–3	Various Colours
Foxglove	Digitalis purpurea	90–120	3–4	Cream, Lavender, Rose, White, Mix
Eucalyptus	Eucalyptus citriodora & E. Gunni	90–180	3–6	Green, Silver
Flowering Kale	Brassica oleracea	60–70	2	Pink, Red, Rose, White, Bicolour
Godetia	Clarkia amoena	75	2½	Pink, Purple, Red
Gomphrena	Gomphrena species	120	4	Pink with Yellow
Hibiscus	Hibiscus	50	1¾	Red, White, Mix

Common Name	Botanical Name	Height		Colour
		cm	ft	
Larkspur	Consolida ambigua	90–120	3–4	Various Colours
Ox-Eye Daisy	Chrysanthemum leucanthemum	60–90	2–3	White with Yellow
Statice + Sea Lavender	Limonium sinuatum + latifolia	60–75	2– 2½	Various Colours
Lisianthus (Texas Blue Bell)	Eustoma grandiflorum	60–115	2–4	Various Colours
Marigold	Tagetes	90	3	Various Colours
Pincushion Flower	Scabiosa caucasica	60	2	Dark Lavender with Silver Center
Snapdragon	Antirrhinum majus	90–150	3–5	Various Colours
Stock	Matthiola incana	80	2–3	Various Colours
Sunflower (Intermediate)	Helianthus	90–150	3–5	Gold, Red, Orange, Yellow
Sunflower (Dwarf)	Helianthus	38–50	1–2	Yellow, Orange
Sunflower (Tall)	Helianthus	150–240	5–8	Various Colours
Sweet Pea	Lathyrus odoratus	45–75	1–3	Various Colours
Trachelium	Trachelium caeruleum	75–105	2½–3	Various Colours
Zinnia	Zinnia elegans	90–120	3–4	Various Colours
Millet (Ornamental)	Pennisetum glaucum	30–120	1–5	Burgundy, Burgundy with green tinges

The language of flowers was a Victorian-era means of communication in which various flowers were used to send coded messages, allowing individuals to express feelings.

Amaranth (Globe) = Immortal Love

Bells of Ireland = Luck

Marigold = Pain and Grief

Sunflower = Pure and Lofty Thoughts

Insects which Feed on Annual Plants in the Prairie Garden
by Terry Galloway

Department of Entomology, Faculty of Agricultural and Food Sciences, University of Manitoba

The seed catalogues are starting to roll in now, and soon you will have all your packets of seeds lined up and ready to go as soon as the May long weekend has passed. You'll have your seedlings growing nicely in their beds and pots and your plans for your summer annuals are perfectly aligned. We always count on a beautiful spring and look forward to the bounty of all those vegetables and the riot of colour provided by flowers. The season is full of promise, except for those pesky insects. If they invade the garden, it will be like a war zone!

When you consider that there are more than 10,000 species of insects in Manitoba, the few dozen that ever feed on your annuals are a very small proportion of the total. We should marvel at their adaptation, the sheer diversity of the insect world, and the adaptations in so many species to feed on plants in almost all stages of growth and on all of their anatomical components. That's small compensation for the damage they can do and the disappointment we feel when that first maggoty radish is pulled from the earth. So here's a sample of some of the insects you might expect as the season develops.

Cutworms: Perhaps the most difficult to deal with are those that are hidden in the soil or in the roots and stems of plants. Cutworms are among the first that we notice that affect our annuals. These moth larvae spend their days hidden in the soil. They come to the surface at night and chew the tender stems of the first seedlings and transplants you put out. They will cut the plant off near the ground level, and may even pull the severed plant down beneath the soil to feed. There are several species that will attack a wide variety of plants. If you dig around the bases of the plants that have been eaten, you can often uncover them, and they will coil themselves up in defence as they lay in your palm while you contemplate their future.

Wireworm larvae are a beautiful golden-orange colour, with six tiny legs behind their head, and a long, tough, cylindrical body behind. These larvae will burrow their way into tubers and larger seeds, causing serious damage only when abundant, usually in soil that has recently been turned into garden from sod. These are the larvae of click beetles. Click beetles are rather elongate and brown, or at least darkly-coloured, and when you turn them over onto their backs they thrash their legs about momentarily before seeming to rest and then produce an audible click and springing into the air with the hope of landing on their feet.

Fly larvae or maggots are legless, creamy white, with their mouth at the tapered end of their body. If you look closely, you will be able to see the dark mouth hooks that they use to excavate their way into their food. Among the most common of these we find in prairie annuals is the cabbage maggot. The adult flies are small, dark grey in colour, without startling features by which to recognize them. But the females lay their eggs in the soil around the stems of crucifers. When the maggots hatch, they penetrate the root, and, if in sufficient numbers, can affect growth in cabbage and cauliflower. They are most annoying when they feed on radishes, creating discoloured tunnels throughout the root. They can have more than one generation per year, so different plantings of radishes may also be susceptible.

Tunnelling insects: Insects which tunnel through our annuals aren't always limited to parts of the plant below the soil surface. The European corn borer is an introduced moth that lays its eggs in tiny, scale-like patches on the leaves of corn. When the larvae hatch, they tunnel their way through the leaves and eventually into the stems of the plant. As long as they stay in the stem, there is little harm done, but too often they make their way into the ears of developing corn as the plant matures. These grayish caterpillars can make their way to the tender kernels to feed, enough to put many people off the damaged ears. Although this pest is most often in corn, they sometimes feed on peppers, where the larvae will be found inside the ripe pepper, with little evidence from the outside that they are there.

Grasshoppers: Most noticeable is when insects feed on the leaves and flowers of a plant. This they accomplish by a number of avenues of attack. These insects can have either chewing or sucking mouthparts. Grasshoppers, for example, have chewing mouthparts; most of our species overwinter as eggs in the soil, laid there in frothy pods. When they invade your garden, they can attack a great variety of plant species, but they always inflict the same kind of damage. They take great gouging bites from the plant, and if they find the plant tasty, they can consume a lot of leaf tissue, especially in their later stages of development. Only adult grasshoppers of most species have wings, and in this stage, they disperse widely, often showing up unexpectedly in your garden later in summer. They may feed on a wide variety of plants, and annuals can suffer serious damage from our more common species. Grasshoppers feed on the leaves and the flowers, and may even chew the stems so that flowers or seed heads can be severed.

Beetles: There are many species of beetles that are occasional pests of annuals in the prairie garden; they too have chewing mouthparts. Flea beetles are small, black beetles that appear on some of the early plants in spring. These beetles overwinter as adults in leaf litter and are usually somewhat host specific. There are several species of crucifer flea beetles that can be extremely abundant. The adult beetles are only a couple of millimetres in total length, but what they lack in size, they can make up for in abundance. They feed on all the cruciferous annuals, including vegetables such as cabbage and brussel sprouts and ornamentals such as nasturtium. The adults chew tiny holes over the entire leaf surface, and when really abundant, reduce the leaves to shreds. Their numbers decline in summer, while they are in the larval stage feeding on the roots of crucifers. However, the next generation emerges in late summer and fall and can have considerable impact on any cruciferous plants still growing in the garden, and just when your nasturtiums are looking their best

There are also flea beetles that attack potatoes, but the impact of these tiny beetles pales in comparison to what can be done by the Colorado potato beetle. These familiar pests are much larger; the adults are cream-coloured with vibrant black stripes down the length of their body. The orange eggs are laid in clusters and hatch into a slug-like larva that also feeds on the leaves. Colorado potato beetles can completely strip the foliage from your potatoes, leaving your rows looking in a very sorry state. If you have ever grown sunflowers in your garden, you may have seen a relative of the Colorado potato beetle feeding on their leaves.

The adult sunflower beetle is a little smaller, but still cream-coloured and with longitudinal black stripes. However, the outermost stripe is interrupted towards the back end, so it looks like an exclamation mark.

Aphids: There are also many insects with sucking mouthparts that feed on annuals in the garden. The most diverse and arguably the most interesting of these are the aphids. There are well over 300 species of aphids recorded in Manitoba, so is it any wonder that we see many of them on our garden annuals? Sometimes they seem to appear out of nowhere and are suddenly very abundant, and are in fact specially adapted to do just that. Aphids produce winged forms that are carried on the wind into the garden. If they land on a suitable host plant, they immediately begin to reproduce. This they do with great efficiency, because during summer, all the winged aphids that arrive are females and they give birth only to live young. All these offspring are female, and they rapidly reach an adult, reproductive stage, whereby they also give birth to live offspring….all females. Aphids have the remarkable ability to reproduce in the absence of males, that is, by parthenogenesis. As a result, tiny colonies of aphids spring up rapidly around those winged dispersers. It is interesting that the initial offspring usually develop into wingless adults which stay put on their host plant and reproduce rapidly to produce several generations of wingless adults. When the plant begins to suffer from aphid attack, or when the aphids become crowded, they begin to produce winged adults, also asexually reproducing females, which fly off to find new host plants. The only time males occur is in fall, when they mate with specialized female forms which will lay eggs that will overwinter, usually on a perennial plant – quite different from those plants they fed upon during summer.

Caterpillars: Of course, there will also be insects attacking your annuals that you might want to encourage in your garden. In recent years, black swallowtail butterflies have been more commonly found throughout the northern parts of their range. These large, beautiful black and yellow butterflies lay their eggs on umbelliferous plants, including carrots, parsnips and dill. The caterpillars grow quite large and are distinctively striped with black,

yellow and green, and they can eat a lot of foliage as they reach maturity. It is certainly worth sacrificing some of your harvest to these lovely creatures. You can easily raise the caterpillars and watch as they develop to the chrysalis stage and ultimately observe the adult butterflies emerging in a container on your kitchen table. If you have never tried this, I highly recommend it; it's something you'll never forget. The black swallowtail isn't the only species of butterfly that feeds on annuals in the garden. If you are really lucky, you may find variegated fritillaries on your pansies. Their spiny caterpillars can consume entire plants, but it's worth it to watch them develop and to have the butterflies flying about the garden, visiting the flowers of other plants you have grown.

This is just a sample of some of the insects we can expect to see on our annuals in the prairie garden this season. Some we consider pests and we apply some form of control to reduce their numbers and to salvage a crop we hope to eat later in the season. Others, though, deserve consideration, so before you decide to eliminate them, think about their place in the garden. Insects are always noteworthy, and will reward those who take time to look at them closely. 🐾

See page 109 for photos.

Benefits of Companion Planting
by Jeannette Adams

Jeannette is a Master Gardener and involved with the Millennium Gardens project and the West Kildonan Horticultural Society in Winnipeg, MB.

Companion planting is the practice of growing plants together so that they have a beneficial effect on one another. The history behind this practice goes back to ancient times and some practices are considered folklore while others have scientific backing. However, the benefits of combining certain crops have been documented in all cultures for many years. Companion planting has been practiced mainly to improve the yield of food crops, but ornamentals also benefit from select groupings.

Interest in companion planting has increased because people are more concerned about the use of chemical fertilizers and pesticides and are looking for more environmentally friendly methods of gardening. There are a number of benefits to consider when deciding whether to try companion planting. Consider that in a natural setting you rarely find vast areas of one type of plant. Instead, you will find a variety of plants that complement one another and co-exist in harmony. In our fields and gardens, it is healthier to have diversity rather than mono-culture because it is less likely that a specific disease or insect will attack all of your plants. By inter-planting a variety of crops you can confuse harmful insects and lure them away from the plants you prefer to grow. Nasturtiums and plants in the cabbage family are attacked by flea beetles. If you prefer one crop over the other, you will plant the lure crop strategically to save the plants you want.

Some plants such as marigolds naturally produce substances that repel certain insects and can be planted near plants that are attacked by those insects. Marigolds, both French and African, have a number of benefits and can be planted throughout your garden. Other plants, such as those in the aster and carrot families help to attract beneficial insects to your yard.

Plants that have long tap roots, even the much maligned dandelion, help to draw soil nutrients up through the soil and deposit them closer to the surface for the use of plants with shorter root systems. Crops in the legume family with their nitrogen fixing ability help to naturally enrich the soil with nitrogen. You will want to know the nutritional needs and root structure of plants in your garden, so that you don't combine all the heavy feeders in the same spot. Practicing crop rotation helps to keep your soil in a more balanced condition.

Some plants, because of their size and structure, provide shade or support. The Native American legend of "The Three Sisters" explains the practice of growing corn, pole beans and squash together. The corn offers support for the beans which replenish the soil and the large leaves of the squash provide living mulch.

Since one of the main reasons to try companion planting is to reduce the use of pesticides in controlling insects and diseases, try planting some of the following throughout your garden. You will have to experiment because some of the newer cultivars may have lost some of their repelling properties.

In general, the more scented varieties are typically more effective. Annuals to inter-plant throughout your garden for their insecticidal effects include: marigolds, geraniums (*Pelargonium*), catnip, nasturtiums, calendulas and petunias. Dusty miller (*Centaurea cineraria*) planted as edging or throughout your beds helps to discourage rabbits. Peppers including ornamental peppers help to protect against some viral diseases. Alliums, chives and onions repel aphids and cabbage butterflies and may discourage black spot. Wormwood (*Artemisia absinthium*) discourages slugs, flea beetles and deer.

Plants that you would want to include in your yard because they attract beneficial insects, butterflies and birds are some of the following: cosmos,

Plant	Compatible	Incompatible
Beans	Beets, carrots, peas, rosemary	Onions, garlic
Beets	Bush beans, cabbage, onions, sage	
Carrots	Lettuce, onions	Dill (stunts growth)
Cucumber	Beans, corn, peas, sunflowers, onions, marigolds	Irish potatoes, aromatic herbs
Eggplant	Beans, spinach, marigolds, catnip	
Lettuce	Chives, garlic, onions (ward off aphids)	
Peas	Carrots, radish, cucumber, corn, beans	Onions, potatoes, gladiolus
Potatoes	Dill, cabbage family	Tomatoes, cucumbers, sunflowers, squash
Squash	Corn, marigolds, nasturtiums	Potatoes
Tomatoes	Basil, onions, parsley, carrots, marigolds	Corn, potatoes, cabbage family (get similar diseases)

zinnia, echinacea, rudbeckias, liatris, milkweed and such herbs as dill, fennel, lovage, borage and chamomile.

Plants to avoid even though they are often listed because of their numerous beneficial qualities are common tansy (*Tanacetum vulgare*) and comfrey (*Symphytum officinale*). These plants are very invasive so unless you can keep them in check, I wouldn't recommend them.

If you are considering planting vegetables and herbs, you may want to consider some of the combinations for the most commonly grown vegetables listed in the preceding chart. The reasons behind these groupings are that either the plants improve growth and flavour, repel insects or discourage shared diseases.

You can create attractive groupings by mixing your annual ornamentals with vegetables and herbs. To achieve success with companion planting, you have to be willing to experiment but you also have to accept that sometimes the rabbits or aphids will win. A diverse garden is a sharing garden. 🐾

Companion Planting
by Ken Land

Ken Land is co-owner of St. Mary's Nursery & Garden Centre.
He has 25 years experience in the lawn and garden industry.

The nicest thing when writing about companion planting is that you are never really wrong. You are talking about a perceived benefit of planting two types of plants in close proximity to one another. If you state that, 'in your opinion', or a 'reliable source' told you, that planting onions in amongst your cabbage will keep cabbage butterflies away, most gardeners will try it and decide for themselves if it provided cabbage butterfly control. There is no real downside to the 'experiment'.

I have heard it said that "marigolds and zinnias grow better if the weed lamb's quarters is plucked from the flowerbed." While not one of the ugliest weeds, I don't envision myself plucking lamb's quarters out of the flowerbed for the next five years just so my marigolds can grow a little more vigorously.

One of the ways companion plants work to protect other plants is by sacrificing themselves for the good of the community. If you plant a border of lettuce such as Red Sails around your flower garden it can act to deter the bunnies from moving further in to your garden. If the bunnies don't show up then you have an attractive, edible, green and red border around your flower garden. The rabbit stops at the lettuce, eats its fill, and moves on, leaving your lilies intact. Nasturtiums can work in much the same sacrificial manner, but with aphids. Nasturtiums are one of the first plants that aphids attack, so can be used as an early warning system that your roses are about to be invaded. If the aphids are not too severe, the nasturtiums can be left to host the aphid population. I am not that tolerant and would likely use some kind of control measure to keep the population in check. This kind of situation is ideal for using ladybug lures. The pheromone lure brings in the local ladybug population who find a thriving food supply inhabiting the nasturtiums. The ladybugs remain as long as the food supply remains. The food supply remains as long as the nasturtiums remain relatively healthy. The roses don't get aphids because they are all on the nasturtiums.

Companion plants can also have insecticidal properties inherent in their make up. French and African Marigolds contain natural bug killers. Interspersing these plants in amongst other flowers greatly discourages a whole host of pests including aphids, flea beetles, and nematodes. Don't like marigolds? Asters, cosmos, chrysanthemums, and coreopsis also fit the bill here.

A number of companion plants work to deter pests because they smell or taste bad to the intended target. Pennyroyal, often called the "No Ant Plant", and spearmint seem to keep ants away. *Coleus canina* (the Scaredy Cat plant or Pee-off plant) is said to discourage cats and dogs from visiting. Hot peppers planted in the garden also repel a number of insects. Catnip discourages flea beetles but attracts cats. Garlic, chives, and allium also discourage insects (some borers) and other pests as well. Citronella geraniums keep mosquitoes at bay. Dusty Miller is said to repel rabbits. As long as they don't keep the gardener away, or deter from the "aesthetics", these plants can be a great addition to the garden.

Legumes that fix nitrogen make any plant growing nearby grow more vigorously if nitrogen levels are low in the soil. In most soils this is often the case, so in most cases there is significant benefit, particularly when the plants are heavy feeders like some petunias. Legumes include, among others, clover, peas, beans, and lupines.

Are there other plants that provide benefit to those grown in association with them? Probably hundreds, and in some cases there is no apparent reason for the benefit. If you find something that works well and looks good, stick with it. There is probably a good reason it works, although nobody may be able to explain it to us. 🦂

See page 109 for photos.

Growing Gladiolus
by Ken Land

Gladiolas are native to Africa, Western Asia, and the Mediterranean. They have been actively hybridized since the early1800's. Today's glads have greatly surpassed their ancestors in beauty, vigour, and variety.

Glads are grown from corms. Each corm produces a small number of cormels during the growing season. Cormels develop into larger corms that will grow to plants that will flower. When two flowers are crossed during pollination, the seed may be collected and grown into corms, which may produce flowers totally unlike either parent. This new plant is a hybrid seedling.

Good soil drainage and full sunlight are necessary to produce good glads. Corms benefit from extra compost and the slight acidity it usually provides. Glads can be planted after the soil can be worked early in the spring. Space your planting out every two weeks for a succession of blooms. Work the soil to a depth of 30 cm (12 in), large corms should be planted 15 cm (6 in) deep, medium corms 10 cm (4 in) and small corms 6 cm (2 in). The first shoots should appear in seven to ten days. When shoots are 8 cm (3 in) tall, use a mulch to moderate soil temperature and retain moisture. A moderate amount of fertilizer heavy in phosphorous and light in nitrogen is recommended. Re-apply when glads reach 15-18 cm (6-7 in) tall. Water regularly throughout their growth and especially during flowering.

Cultivate the soil to keep down weeds and thoroughly aerate the root area. Cultivation should not be too deep or the shallow roots may be injured.

Gladiolus is the longest lasting of all cut flowers. The flower spike is in the centre of the plant and it will continue to elongate above the plant until it has reached its full bloom. Soon after cutting, spikes require their stems to be immersed in water. Spikes may be cut with one floret open and unopened florets will continue to open. Leave four or five leaves on the plant to allow corms to continue to develop.

Gladiolus, like any other plant, has its natural enemies. Aphids, thrips, and tarnished plant bugs, are among the more common insect problems on glads. Botrytis Blight, Fusarium Yellows, and numerous viral diseases can also affect glads.

Aphid damage to the plant is visible in a distortion and yellowing of the leaves and flowers. Aphids also excrete "honeydew" which can coat the plant with a shiny, sticky, ant attracting substance. In the spring wingless, fertile, female aphids hatch from over wintering eggs in what will be the first of many generations over the growing season.

Thrip damage to glads first appears as silvery white stripes on both the flowers and foliage. Flowers often become deformed and discoloured and the foliage eventually browns and dies. Thrips have rasping mouths that tear off the outer layers of plant tissue to allow them to feed on sap. Freezing winter temperatures typically prevent thrips from over wintering. They winter on stored bulbs or are transported up from the south. Eggs are inserted directly into growing plant tissue and once hatched, it takes 2 to 4 weeks for a thrip to mature enough to start the cycle over again.

Tarnished Plant Bugs pierce the plant tissue to feed on the cell contents. A tan or bleached spot is the result of this feeding. Abnormal development or flower bud blast may also result from feeding. Like most sucking insects, they make great vectors for viruses.

Botrytis Blight causes leaf and flower lesions, and stem and corm rot in glads. Leaf lesions have brown or grey centres covered with grey masses of spores. As the disease progresses, leaves and stem yellow and die. Other disease symptoms include small water spots that brown over time on the edge of the flower petals. Corms harvested during wet weather can become infected with the disease. Cool, rainy weather further encourages the spread of the disease.

Stunted foliage and stunted S-shaped flower spikes characterize Fusarium Yellows. Yellowing starts on the leaf tips, spreading throughout the plant until it is dead. When lifted, infected corms are spotted with circular, firm, brown lesions. Fusarium Yellows survives on diseased corms and for several years in contaminated soil.

Numerous viral diseases can infect glads. A wide range of symptoms from streaked, mottled, or spotted leaves can indicate the presence of a virus. When infected corms are planted, insects can rapidly spread the virus. Thrip damage to glads is often mistaken for virus damage.

Dig corms for storing six to eight weeks after blooming (or as long as weather permits). If disease or thrips were problematic, it may be easier to dispose of the dug corms rather than risk reintroducing the problem from stored corms. Collect the smaller cormels to replant to increase stock. Twist off the foliage and put corms in a dry, airy place to dry for approximately two weeks. Clean corms of old roots and store in a cool airy place for the winter. Remember the new corms are produced on top of the original; the old corm is thrown away. Dusting the corms with a combination insecticide/fungicide is recommended.

See page 100 for photos.

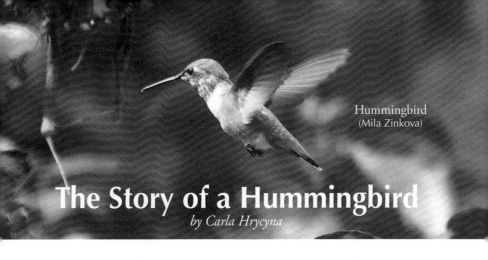

Hummingbird
(Mila Zinkova)

The Story of a Hummingbird
by Carla Hrycyna

With every garden comes a story or perhaps two from its hardworking and diligent creator – yes, the gardener. We all do it. We love to speak of the different seasons and occasions we hold in our yards. As well, we speak boastfully of our successes in our gardens, and are just as quick to lend a comment or two to the unsuccessful gardening experiences. I, like all of you, love to relate my enthusiasm for gardening, and have done so for the past decade. So, I will begin by telling you a 'story' befitting this topic.

Years ago our daughter, who was just turning four, would help in the garden whenever her curiosity led her there. She loved the garden, digging and planting the flowers with me (more precisely, she probably loved the wet soil more than the flowers). When spring turned to summer, she would lie on the floor at the front door and look out to the lovely collage of containers that dressed our front walkway. The flowers were bursting from their pots in full glory and I thought, "Yes, she loves the flowers!" On a few occasions, I asked if she would like to help me with the flowers and for a while the response was always "NO!" Strange! After some prodding, she admitted not wanting to play outside and help with the flowers because "the mosquitoes are too big." An explanation of mosquitoes did not ease her fear of the nasty pest. It was not until days later when she again lay on the foyer floor gazing at the beautiful pots that she called to me to come and see 'the huge mosquitoes'. This brought us both to the foyer floor where I patiently waited for her to show me the mosquitoes. However, instead of a mosquito, she showed me a hummingbird.

How could we have hummingbirds? We lived in a new neighbourhood with very few trees, shrubs or gardens. The answer was not the maturity of the trees, shrubs, perennials, and annuals, but rather the varieties that attracted them to our garden.

Let it be known—supply the nectar for hummingbirds and they will come!

Artificial nectar in the form of a colourfully tinted red, syrupy liquid held in a suspended vessel, will attract hummingbirds to this artificial food source. My personal preference is to use plants with their natural nectars to attract these amazing fast flying birds. With wings that flutter as fast as 55–75 times a second, Ruby-throated hummingbirds (*Archilochus colubris*) can be commonly found in Manitoba. Their heartbeat (up to 1200 beats per second) takes up a huge amount of their energy. Hummingbirds weigh very little, about 5 grams/0.176 ounces and can fly up to 100 km (62 miles) per hour. They appear to be held suspended in mid-air when hovering to sample the nectar from sweet flowers. Their high-energy requirement does not just come from flower nectar, but from ingesting spiders and smaller insects.

Hummingbirds can be found in woodlands, parks, and flower gardens and will travel great distances for food. Planting specific flowers will encourage hummingbirds to venture into your garden. Hummingbirds buzzing from one favourable flower to another assist in the natural pollination of certain plants.

Hummingbird Flowers

For a flower to attract a hummingbird it must have three things: 1) The flowers must be suited to accommodate the long billed beak of the hummingbird. 2) The flowers must be brightly coloured to attract the hummingbird. 3) The blooms must be able to produce sufficient nectar to feed the bird.

Nicotiana alata (Flowering Tobacco) belongs to the genus of the *Solananceae* or nightshade family and ranges in height from ⅓–1½ m (1–5 ft) tall. Trumpeted star-shaped blooms are either held above the foliage or dangle slightly on a downward angle. I find *Nicotiana* 'sylvestris' the most scented followed by *Nicotiana* 'Perfume' varieties. The fragrances are strongest in the evening air. Colours range from pure white, to chartreuse green ('Saratoga Lime'), to soft pink ('Starmaker Lime') to two-tone purple ('Saratoga Purple Bi-colour). *Nicotiana* is best grown in full sun to part shade.

Torenia (also known as the 'Wishbone flower' or 'Bluewings') is a beautiful trumpeted flower 2½–5 cm (1–2 in) long in shades of purple, lavender, pinks and yellows. Favourable to shady locations, the plant form is dense in habit with toothed pointed leaves. *Torenia* is perfect for hanging baskets and container plantings.

Morning Glories are available in dwarf varieties such as 'Royal Ensign' as well as ramblers (climbers), *Ipomoea tricolour* 'Heavenly Blue' with sky blue flowers climbing 3½ m (12 ft) tall, and *Ipomoea* x *imperialis* 'Sunrise Serenade' with its large double ruffled cherry blooms. This Japanese variety is superb for garden performance. 'Sunrise Serenade' blooms from early summer to frost, with the flowers lasting longer than older varieties.

Whether bush type or climbing, Morning Glories belong to the family of *Convolvulaceae*. They favour a location with full sun and good drainage. Older varieties have short-lived blooms (lasting only a day) ranging in colours from deep blues, scarlet, and soft pink. Try planting it in combination with *Ipomoea* 'Moon Flower'. *Ipomoea* 'Moon Flower', like morning glories, has similar 7½ cm (3 in) blooms, gracing climbing vines that open during the evening hours, the reverse of the morning glory. Grow in full sun for best performance.

Verbena – can either be purchased for its upright habit (*Verbena* 'Imagination') for bedding use, or for its semi-cascading form, ideal for hanging baskets and container plantings (*Verbena* 'Temari'). *Verbena* is available in reds, purples, pinks and yellow shades.

Nasturtiums (*Tropaeolum majus*)- probably the easiest flower to grow. These bedding and climbing plant varieties will thrive in 'not the best' garden soil and grow very easily. Hot summer shades of orange, red and cream will entice any hummingbird to your yard. These edible flowers will be extremely attractive to the hummingbirds once you have found the perfect blend. 'Alaska Mix' grows to 30 cm (12 in) tall with white marbled foliage and a single bloom, while 'Jewel Mix' is as tall with a semi-double bloom.

Whichever flowers you choose to entice hummingbirds to your garden, just remember to have a good supply of flowers for them to sample the nectar. It is beneficial to also supply a shallow pool of water for them to use.

A magical fluttering of hummingbird wings is mesmerizing to gardeners, and inspires us to enhance our gardens with the colourful plants essential to the hummingbird's existence. 🐦

Flowers to Attract Hummingbirds
(just to mention a few)

Annuals		Perennials	
Gladiolas	Fuchsia	*Agastache*	
Lantana	Hibiscus	*Lonicera* 'Honeysuckle' Vine	
Mandevilla	Petunia	Monarda	
Salvia	*Calibrochoa*	*Campsis radicans*	
Cuphea	*Cleome*	Columbine	
Snapdragons			

Popular Poppies
by Frances Wershler

Oriental Poppy 'Patty's Plum' (Fran Wershler)

There are 19 genera, over 120 species, 22 in the genus Papaver alone, in the poppy family *Papaveraceae*. You may have heard of, seen, or grown them. They may be annual, biennial or perennial and most are hardy, tough plants growing in the temperate climates of Africa, North America and Eurasia.

Several species in the family are perennial including some in the genus *Papaver:* the Oriental poppy (*Papaver orientale)* and the Alpine poppy (*Papaver alpinum*). In the genus *Meconopsis* is the Himalayan blue Poppy, a perennial many people in zones 2 and 3 try to grow. The Matilija poppy or *Romneya coulteri*, (sometimes called 'fried egg poppy') is a member of the genus *Romneya*. This perennial is native to California and only grows in extremely hot, dry places, while *Meconopsis*, on the other hand, prefers cool growing conditions like in early spring or at high altitudes, but it will grow in our prairie gardens with a little care and the addition of gritty soil.

All oriental poppy cultivars grow well on the Prairies: a white poppy with a dark purple blotch called Royal Wedding, a salmon-pink dark-eyed one called Princess Victoria Louise, and a newer dark maroon-plum toned poppy called Patty's Plum. Vesey's catalogue lists Black poppy (*Papaver somniferum),* as one for those people fascinated with dark and black flowers. It is fully double and a very deep red colour. The Oriental poppy we most often see is a red-orange, single or semi-double form with a black blotch, commonly known as Brilliant poppy.

In my own garden the Brilliant poppy will overtake all surrounding areas if I allow it, but Patty's Plum took five years to bloom, produced five blooms and was back to its blue-green jagged leaves in a week. In its 6th year in 2009 it had 6 blooms. The foliage of the Oriental poppy dies off late in summer and in extremely long open autumns will reemerge and bloom briefly once more.

Delicate Iceland poppies, (*Papaver nudicaule), and some of the opium poppies, (*Papaver somniferum*), are biennials. Some gardeners manage to grow Iceland poppies in sandy areas by sowing seed in late fall or early spring or by purchasing plants from a greenhouse. Unless the plants come into flower and set seed, the process has to be repeated. Garden writers suggest that Icelandic poppies seeded in autumn are the strongest.

Easy-to-grow annual poppies include the California poppy, (*Papaver californicum), known for its rich gold, orange and red-orange tones, and *Papaver rhoeas,* which includes the Corn poppy, the Shirley poppy, and the Field poppy, or Red poppy. Many of these have four red petals that look like crinkled silk with a central black splotch. The Shirley poppy may be found in a variety of pastel colours and double types. It was created around 1880 by a vicar of the parish of Shirley, England. In a corner of his garden the vicar found one poppy with a white border around its petals, a variant of surrounding field poppies. His work

in selection produced a strain of poppies ranging in colour from pink and red to pale mauve and white, none of which had the usual black blotches. Any one of this group is easily grown from seed as an annual for a showy note in the garden, very often appearing in successive years in spite of efforts to remove the plants' seed pods. The seed may be sown in summer for bloom the following spring as it requires a cold treatment before germination. All of these poppies are excellent pollen sources for bees.

The bright red Corn poppy is so called because all early grains were referred to as 'corn' and this poppy grew where ground was tilled to grow grains. It has been associated with wartime remembrance. 'In Flanders Fields', a poem by Canadian soldier, John McRae, immortalized those World War I soldiers on the Western Front where red poppies bloomed as war distressed the soil. It is typical that poppy seeds may lie dormant for years until the soil is disturbed and then suddenly spring into life, just as it happened in Europe, shooting up numerous plants with showy terminal flowers on hairy stalks. The poppy symbol is now worn on lapels across Canada for November 11, Remembrance Day, to honor veterans and war dead.

Another red poppy is the Welsh poppy, (*Meconopsis cambric),* which originates and grows in England, Wales and Ireland.

Double poppies such as the Opium poppy (*Papaver somniferum*), may or may not be of the type that is used to extract opium and several other refined opiates or sleep inducers including morphine and codeine. In seed catalogues the word *somniferum* is sometimes omitted, using rather the word *paeoniflorum*, referring to the peony-like flowers. This is probably a sub-type of opium poppy with very double flowers in a wide range of attractive colours. The flowers are deeply lobed and ruffly so that sometimes catalogues refer to them as 'pompom'. For generations these poppy seeds have been important food items and contain healthy oils used worldwide in the culinary arts. The T&T Seeds catalogue puts one of these poppies in its herb section with the reference "pretty flowers produce large pods loaded with tasty seeds. Ideal for baking cakes, breads." Winnipeg's Sage Garden Herbs lists Opium poppy, (*Papaver somniferum*), with the description "lavender coloured flowers produce tasty blue poppy seeds that are traditionally used in baking." Many catalogues prefer not to use the term '*somniferum*' and some will not ship the seeds for this poppy within the United States. It is considered a noxious weed in 46 states.

Canada's Controlled Drugs and Substances Act prohibits possession of *Papaver somniferum* for illegal purposes, however, it exempts that poppy's seeds in its list of prohibitions.

All poppies exude a white, latex-like fluid when the stem, bud or leaf is cut. In countries where opium is collected the pods are slashed and the drying fluid is later scraped off for processing. The leaves and latex have an acrid taste and are mildly poisonous to grazing animals. The escaping fluid makes poppies wilt if used in flower arrangements so knowledgeable flower arrangers choose a poppy bud and seal the end of a cut stem with a flame or by dipping the stem ends in boiling water.

From the glorious array of bright poppies there has to be at least one that will attract each flower gardener. Choose a mannerly perennial poppy that comes up in the same spot each year, or be brave and plant a few seeds of the Shirley, Welsh, or California poppy. Enjoy the colour the first year, then look for seedlings next year. All you need is one pod to produce a few little plants. Weed out the poppies popping up in undesirable spots. Just enjoy their bright tissue paper look as they attract the bees and move in the breeze. 🐝

See page 110 for photos.

The New Garden Complex at the International Peace Garden

by Douglas Hevenor

Doug is the CEO of the International Peace Gardens, a 2,339 acre Botanical Garden on the Canada – U.S. border at Boissevain, Manitoba

If you begin with the words… serene… quiet… still… cool… calm... and silent, eventually you acquire peace—and what better place to achieve it than in a garden—our very own the International Peace Garden (IPG).

The Garden, located on the international border between North Dakota and Manitoba near the towns of Dunseith, ND, and Boissevain, MB, was originally conceived in 1928 by Dr. Henry J. Moore, a Canadian horticulturist and teacher from Islington, Ontario. While attending a gathering of gardeners in Greenwich, Connecticut, Dr. Moore conceived the idea of creating a garden on the international boundary, "where the people of the two countries could share the glories found in

a lovely Garden and the pleasures found in warm friendship."

Dr. Moore sought to create a living memorial to everlasting peace between two nations; a thing of supreme beauty and an inspiration to the hearts of all humanity. The garden was commemorated on July 14, 1932. In many ways, the intent of the early visionaries of this garden was to create a second "Garden of Eden". It was proposed that the Garden would physically be one of the largest and most beautiful in the

The Floral Clock at the IPG (Carla Hrycyna)

world, and include plants that were native to each country, greenhouses and conservatory, individual gardens of different styles and purposes, a radio station to broadcast globally messages of peace and brotherhood, and a school for the education and training in 'gardening'. (Moore, Sept. 1929).

Many histories have been written about the IPG describing the development of the garden, the creation of children's music and athletic camps and the participation of many of the fraternal organizations that have worked exhaustively over the years to enhance the IPG. In 2001, the Board of Directors and the Executive Director of the IPG, embarked on an extensive study to expand the Peace Mandate at the IPG.

With the support of the Canadian Federal Government, they undertook an extensive 3-part study of the region, the site, and its proposed improvement. Through their consultants, Gaboury Préfontaine Perry architectes, Winnipeg, MB, they have developed a concept and plans for the expansion of the IPG's facilities and programs. A key part of this new initiative is the related expansion of the Interpretative Centre, the Gardens and the construction of a conservatory.

The Garden Complex – IPG's Key Marketing Focus

The IPG Board has decided that the development of the Interpretive Centre and Conservatory (IC&C) and garden complex is the IPG's unique selling point (USP). Friesen Tokar Architects, Landscape, and Interior Designers of Winnipeg, MB will provide the final IC&C Design for the building with DeCloet Greenhouse Construction suppling the Conservatory roof design and glazing.

Focusing on the garden, together with appropriate interpretive development, is the best strategy to attract potential visitors to drive the significant distances from major centres and the seasonality of the location. A garden that is simply a 'bunch of pretty flowers' will not be sufficiently unique to capitalize on the garden's potential as a destination location and to serve the objectives of the Centre.

There are many lovely botanical centres in both the US and Canada that are a 'must see' when someone is in that city or region. However, they are usually not the sole reason that the public would visit a specific area. In order for the IPG garden complex to be a 'must see' in its own right (and to overcome distance and seasonality), the IPG will develop the garden to be a unique and substantive garden complex that is integrally linked to the IC&C objectives and activities.

For example, it is expected that some of the programming will formally integrate the use of the gardens and that all of those who attend or participate in the IC&C's programs will feel the influence of the gardens. The building design

International Peace Garden's
Sunken Garden Planting Plan
(Charles Anderson Landscape Architecture)

also enhances the influence of nature and the gardens even when indoors.

The IC&C will exhibit the clear connection between the garden and its historic role in promoting peace. Throughout history, the garden has symbolized the ideal world or paradise, a place for rebirth and regeneration, a refuge from stress and upheaval – very much the place to find peace and resolve conflict. By expanding on the garden's relationship to interpretation and learning, the IC&C will create a substantive basis on which to build a 'must see' destination facility.

The Garden Complex

The vision for the formal garden is described as a 'garden complex' because the concept involves a series of gardens and interpretive components, rather than one garden site. Charles Anderson and Associates Landscape Architects of Seattle, WA created the current design honouring the design concepts of the past and telling the story of recent plant introduction to the Prairie landscape.

Together with interpretation and explanation of the rationale for the style of garden and its significance, we will focus in particular on how gardens and plants contribute to peace and tranquillity. Anderson is formally from Jamestown, ND and part of his design team is from Winnipeg, MB.

Len's Landscaping, a member of the Manitoba Landscape Nursery

Trade from Winkler, MB, is installing the landscape plant material and decorative fountains. Swanberg Construction from Valley City, ND, is installing all the concrete walkways within the garden complex.

The following are only a few examples of the types of gardens that will be analysed during the final design phase as to their suitability and potential role for inclusion in the garden complex:

The Living Fence - Comprised of a new selection and introduction (2008) of a columnar flowering crab 'Purple Splendour' introduced by Jeffries Nurseries, Portage La Prairie, MB. Another new introduction, 'Gladiator' will also be featured. This burgundy coloured flowering crab is also a very columnar selection. Jeffries Nurseries' research and development program has released 23 outstanding varieties, with many more in the works. Northern Garden Introductions have been selected and evaluated under harsh prairie conditions and offer many outstanding ornamental features.

Rose Garden - A comprehensive collection of Hardy Shrub Roses. These Explorer roses originally developed at the Ottawa research station, with new Canadian Artist varieties being introduced from the research station in l'Assomption, PQ. The Parkland series are another exceptional series of hardy Canadian roses, developed by the Morden Research Station in southern Manitoba. We will also display 'Easy Elegance' roses bred at Bailey's Nursery of Minnesota and the Buck roses bred at Iowa State University. All are very hardy with exceptional blooms.

Shrub Collections - This collection will highlight new introductions for the Prairies from North Dakota State University, as well as introductions from the Morden Research Station in Manitoba and the Indian Head Research Farm in Saskatchewan.

Perennial Selections - The garden floor will be carpeted with a very diverse selection of hardy perennials. The collection will highlight the Perennial Plant of the Year Selections and provide visitors with a living library of plant material to evaluate for use in their home gardens. The perennials will be supplied by Aubin Nurseries in Carmen, MB, Jeffries Nurseries in Portage La Prairie, MB and T & T Seeds in Winnipeg, MB.

Arboretum - Here we will showcase recent introductions, new selections, and potential trial plants for zone 3B.

Spring Bulbs - This garden will provide the visitor with a comprehensive collection of hardy spring bulbs including: Tulip, Daffodil, Hyacinth, Crocus, Anemone, Grape Hyacinth, and Siberian Squill. The bulbs will be located within the sunken garden area and they will be fenced and protected from browsing deer and moose.

Summer Bulbs - The collection will feature the genus *Lilium*. This genus, of about 110 species, is in the lily family (*Liliaceae*). Lilies are important as large showy cold hardy perennial flowering garden plants that make great cut flowers, and provide gorgeous colour shows during most of the summer season. Most lily species are reliably hardy as low as Zone 3. There are about 80 species and several hundred cultivars available ranging in height from $\frac{2}{3}$–$2\frac{1}{2}$ m (2–8 ft). They are available in white, yellow, red, pink, orange, maroon, and bi-colours.

Given prairie environmental conditions, adapted plant material will have to be used in place of non-native species in some of the gardens. Recognizing the constraints placed on the garden complex by climate, the IC&C will play an important role in supplementing the visitors' learning experience regarding the physical garden and plant material – especially in telling the story of the gardens during the 'off-season'.

Additionally, the IC&C will be able to educate and inform visitors about aspects of the garden complex story that cannot be done in the physical garden because of climatic/plant material constraints. There is great potential for the Conservatory and the opportunity may exist for expansion at the south end of the building. The space will include a varied collection of tropical plants focusing on Palms and Succulents. The collection will be connected with a vast array of tropical foliage and

highlighted with Orchids, Brome-
liads, and many distinct Succulents
and Cactus. Winter visitors will have
the opportunity to stroll through this
tropical oasis located near the Garden
Complex above the frozen prairie.

The IC&C will indeed act as the
"knowledge gateway" for visitors that
are looking for information regarding
the IPG history, facilities, and programs. In addition, this area will act as
the delivery space for travelling exhibits from across the USA and Canada.
Other amenities that will be part of
the Interpretive Centre will include
restaurant/coffee shop facilities, visitor
orientation/interpretation facilities,
and a new gift/souvenir shop.

In addition, the IC&C will
include stories regarding the roles
that gardens have played throughout
history in peace or conflict resolution, as well as, explanations of
some basic landscape design theories
regarding how the placement of
shape, size, and colour can affect the
'feeling' of a garden. Here, we will
be able to share the rich history and
heritage of many different facets of
prairie life, including the research
and development of ornamental
plants and the role plants played
with respect to culinary, medicinal,
and spiritual uses by Native people
and settlers to the prairie.

A key objective of this 'market-
ing strategy' is to develop a significant educational component that
will make people want to come to
visit the IPG to learn about the role

of gardens in human development,
rather than only to learn about
gardening. This strategy will provide many opportunities to weave
messages about peace and conflict
resolution into the information
about the historical and cultural
significance of gardens.

In addition to an educational
experience, the garden will offer a
variety of places for individuals to
contemplate the role that gardens
could play in their own lives and in
the lives of nations, as well as a place
for contemplation, stress relief and
conflict resolution. We encourage
you to come, visit the Peace Garden, and enjoy the changes that our
garden complex has provided.

Contact Us
Canada
International Peace Garden
Box 419
Boissevain, MB R0K 0E0
Phone (204) 534-2510

United States
International Peace Garden
10939 Highway 281
Dunseith, ND 58329
Phone (701) 263-4390
Fax (701) 263-316

Phone Toll Free: (888) 432-6733
www.peacegarden.com

Zantedeschia aethiopica
(Sandy Venton)

Pond Plants
by Ken Land

Botanists do not classify aquatic plants separately from other plants, despite their unique growth habits. Adaptations by some species of plants to grow in water is what allows them to become pond plants. Some species, which can be purchased as pond plants, like *Lysimachia nummularia* (Creeping Jenny), can also be found in the perennial department and in the hanging basket trailer section of a garden centre.

While there are a number of different ways to categorize pond plants we try to keep it fairly simple. There are the oxygenators – plants that absorb carbon dioxide from the water in significant quantities and give off oxygen. Marginal or bog plants consist of plants grown in shallow water, often around the edges of the pond. They make up the largest grouping of pond plants and contain plants that flower, plants grown for their leaf texture, trailers, tall varieties, short varieties,

etc. A third grouping is the floaters. As the name implies, this group consists of non–anchored plants like duckweed. Finally, we give the *Nymphaea* (water lilies) a group all to themselves.

Water lilies love full sun but require a minimum of six hours of direct sunlight each day in order to bloom. Planted at the bottom of the pond, lilies prefer calm water in order to thrive. The foliage on the surface can play a key role in creating a natural balance in the pond by providing shade for the pond. Water lilies can be grouped into two categories: tropical and hardy. Tropical water lilies will not survive in water whose temperature goes below 18° C (65° F), so only the real adventurous in Winnipeg attempt these. 'Lilies of the Nile' are plants that have highly toothed foliage and a vast array of rich coloured flowers. They bloom all summer long on stalks that stretch 10–13 cm (4–5 in) above the water. Hardy water lilies (zone 3 and up) are available in a rainbow of colours. My favourite is the Burgundy Princess. With deep red 10–13 cm (4–5 in) flowers and small maroon leaves that age to dark green, it is truly spectacular. Wintering lilies can be a challenge. As long as your pond doesn't become a block of ice over the winter, hardy water lilies can be left in. I have heard of someone going to the trouble of laying plywood, plastic, and flax straw over their pond to ensure their pond did not freeze solid. Other ways to winter your water lilies include: storing them in a plastic bag in the 'beer fridge' in the basement, burying and mulching them (60 cm/24 in deep) in the garden outside, putting them in a plastic bag filled with moist peat, and storing in a cool location in the basement, or growing them in the kids wading pool in a sunny location. I find the 'fridge' solution will yield the best overall results.

Like the water lilies above, floaters provide shading for the pond below. Cooling the water, hiding the fish, providing a place to spawn, and providing a healthy meal for a hungry koi, floaters greatly benefit the pond. The two most popular are *Pistia stratoides* (water lettuce) and *Eichornia crassipes* (water hyacinth). Water lettuce has a unique, light green colour to it. It grows best in light shade and moving water. Water hyacinth has a distinctive upright leaf and lilac–blue flowers. Lesser Duckweed (*Lemna minor*) and Fairy Moss (*Azolla caroliniana*) are a couple of 'rampant' growers. Weed is the operative word in duckweed. If you don't have the fish to keep the population in check (consumption levels need to be high), your pond will quickly become a green carpet of these two floaters. In moderate amounts, these plants can enhance the beauty of your pond. Winter your floaters in the compost pile, and replace them with new ones each spring. "They looked good until…" is the most common phrase heard from those who avoided tossing the plant in the fall.

Oxygenators help provide an environment in which your fish can flourish. They act as natural filters and actively compete for nutrient in the pond with algae. While Horn-

(Sandy Venton)

wort (*Ceratophyllum demersum*) is the most common oxygenator, other species are available. These plants are generally submerged, although some have foliage that will float on the surface. *Myriophyllum* (water milfoil) have attractive lacy foliage, the *brasiliensis* (Red Stemmed Parrots Feather) species have an unusual red stem. *Elodea canadensis* (American or Canadian Waterweed or Pondweed) produces a dainty white bloom that floats on the water surface while the feathery foliage remains entirely underwater.

Marginals are generally planted anywhere from 2.5–20 cm (1–8 in) deep, depending on species. The choices in the grouping are huge. Heights, flower colour, growth habit, zones 2 through 10, variegated foliage, grasses, just about anything you want. Some of my favourites include:

• *Colocasia esculenta* 'Black Magic' – At 1½–1.8 m (5–6 ft) tall this purple leaved elephant ear makes a bold statement in any pond.
• *Cyperus alternifolius* 'Gracillis'– Umbrella–like whorls of green foliage top the short hollow stems of this 60 cm (24 in) tall graceful looking plant.
• *Hibiscus coccineus* – The large brilliant red flowers on this plant make it stand out in the pond.
• *Canna* 'Pretoria' – Hard to choose between canna lily varieties, but the huge melon–orange blooms and zebra striped foliage of yellow and

green make this 1¼ m (4 ft) tall plant a giant in the pond.
• *Juncus effusus* 'Spiralis' – Corkscrew rush, with it's thin spiralling leaves make this plant an unusual pond feature.
• *Lysimachia nummularia* 'Aurea' – Creeping Jenny, with it's trailing habit make this an ideal plant to trail into or out of a pond to hide and soften the edges.
• *Zantedeschia aethiopica* – With the graceful large white flowers, this calla lily makes a great addition to the pond.

Irises, Marsh marigolds, lobelia, rushes and others too numerous to mention, can all blend together to create the perfect wetland habitat. Wintering marginals depends on the zone of the plant you have and the zone you are in. I find those plants capable of wintering in your zone do best if the container is planted in an empty spot in the garden under a good mulch.

Like your flower garden, planning which plant to put where, is the key ingredient in developing a gorgeous pond. All the same plant features must be considered (height, texture, bloom period, …) when developing that plan. Or you could just pick up a few of those "aquabaskets" where the expert has already put together three or four pond plant varieties that look great together. 🦜

See page 108 for a photo.

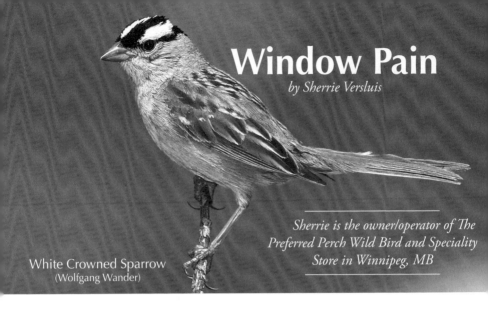

Window Pain

by Sherrie Versluis

Sherrie is the owner/operator of The Preferred Perch Wild Bird and Speciality Store in Winnipeg, MB

White Crowned Sparrow
(Wolfgang Wander)

Songbird populations are one of the greatest concerns of the world today. Their constantly declining numbers are attributed to several issues, including habitat loss, changing weather patterns, chemicals, and two very suburban problems, free-roaming cats and window collisions. The latter two are responsible for literally millions of deaths per day of songbirds across North America. They are two of the most easily correctable problems, yet each poses its own difficulty in achieving any success.

During the spring and fall migrations each year, millions of songbirds migrate across the continent, crossing many dangerous paths. Everything from wind turbines to power lines, communication towers to vehicle collisions, and stray cats to window panes, contribute to songbird deaths. Dr. Daniel Klem of Muhlenberg College in Allentown, PA, who has studied window colli-

sions for 20 years, has concluded that windows kill more birds than any other human factor. In total he has found that about 900 million birds die every year just from window collisions. In comparison, vehicle collisions account for another 50-100 million deaths, communication towers for 4-10 million, pesticides for 67 million, and electric transmission lines are up to 174 million bird deaths. With numbers like that it makes you wonder how we even have any birds left! This is why it is so important to try to do what you can to minimize bird deaths around you. Reconsider chemical applications around your yard, try to keep habitat as natural as possible, don't unnecessarily cut trees, and do something about your windows if you are experiencing window collisions.

To stop birds from hitting windows you must obstruct the reflection that birds are seeing. Many people try to prevent collisions by hanging something like a stained glass piece in the window.

Unfortunately, nothing on the inside of the glass will help. If birds could see beyond the reflections they would see right into our homes and would never fly into the window. Closing blinds sometimes works, but depending on the type of windows you have, it just might increase the problem. The answer is to put something on the outside of the glass. The most popular options are static cling decals that come in two different options. One type of decal is a silhouette of a bird of prey. These decals are black in colour and do not scare birds away from your yard. Birds only see these as they are approaching your window, then swerve out of the way to avoid impact.

Window Alerts are an ultra-violet decal that has a glowing effect birds are able to see. To the human eye it just looks like a shadow of an image on the glass. These decals are available in the shapes of hummingbirds, butterflies, and maple leafs. The concept of these decals is not the shape but the fact that they glow on the window indicating to birds there is an object to avoid. The only thing to remember about this type of decal is that they do fade within a year and require replacement in order to be effective. If a bird hits your window and does end up flying away, in most cases it still dies as a result of head injuries, which is why it is so important to eliminate the problem.

It is difficult to prevent window collisions based on the placement of plants in the yard. If the window is not reflecting your plants it will probably show the sky and other surroundings which will still cause collisions. Placing a shepherds hook with hanging baskets about 1¼–1½ cm (4-5 ft) from the window would be helpful if you don't mind a slightly obstructed view. This will at least help to eliminate a full flight path into the window and reduce the strength of the impact if it doesn't completely deter them.

Free-roaming cats are a very heated topic among cat owners and those who deal with stray cats in their yards. Defecating in gardens, territorial spraying in yards, or killing birds at birdfeeders are just some of the complaints associated with roaming cats. It is a subject that can escalate into serious neighbourhood wars with each side having very strong opinions.

Even though most cats are well looked after at home they still hunt and kill birds and in most cases it's just for the sake of the hunt. Millions of young birds, as well as ground-nesting birds, are killed by cats. When birds are injured by cats, they can die a prolonged death due to bacterial infections they get from cat teeth and claws. It is estimated that *every single day* in North America, 5-10 million songbirds are killed by cats.

Many cat owners who allow their cats to roam have the belief that it is the natural instinct of cats to hunt and roam. They are indeed correct, however, domestic cats are not an indigenous species here in North America. They were introduced as a domestic pet, not as a free-roaming animal. The problem with their roaming has created many problems. There are now many diseases among cats that never existed until roaming numbers became epidemic. Feline leukemia, FIV, and FIP are just a few of the contagious ailments that are among cats now. There have been many unnecessary deaths among cats like poisoning (accidental and intentional) and deaths by predators such as the city dwelling Great-horned owl which regularly dines on cats, road-kill, and even by wandering into a yard where a large dog may live.

Those who own cats should keep them where they are safe. It does not mean your cat can't enjoy the outdoors: get a leash and harness, or build an outdoor run with cat scratchers built in. This can increase the lifespan of your cat and reduce vet bills dramatically throughout their lifetime.

For gardeners, songbirds play a huge role in a healthy garden. They are Nature's insect controllers, pollinators, seed planters, and provide the sweet songs that fill our ears as we tend to our yards and gardens. Continued decline of bird numbers of this magnitude is absolutely unacceptable! Many cities, like Winnipeg, have enacted by-laws about roaming cats, but enforcement is limited. Groups informing the public about window collisions have been started throughout North America to educate businesses and homeowners on how they can assist in preventing injury or death resulting from window collisions.

Please make an effort to assist songbirds in making a comeback by doing your part, whether it's by changing your habits about your pets, reducing chemical usage in your yard, or just spreading the word to those who don't know how to deal with some of these issues. We, as individuals, may not be able to resolve all songbird issues on our own, but, doing what we can in our yards, is a first important step. 🐦

Try a different lettuce

Mesclun – It's a seed mixture of many leaf lettuce types. Plant and pick while small. **Mini head lettuce** – like Tom Thumb. Each tiny head makes a serving. **Red Deer Tongue** – a red lettuce with a sweet flavour. **Red Sails** – A ruffled, red leaved variety that is fast growing. **Butter lettuce** – the most subtle flavoured lettuce.

Musings of a Zone 1 Gardener

by Darm Crook

Darm Crook is a retired carpenter living and gardening in Zone 1, nine kilometres south of Hay River, NWT. He is also a plant hybridizer.

Lisianthus
*A North American
wild flower native to Texas*

Contrary to popular belief, Lisianthus is a tender, short lived perennial. It is not an annual, as such. It is slow to start from seed and takes about seven to nine months to first flower. Therefore, seed should be planted in late October or early November for flowering in June and July. Every thing about them is slow, slow and slower. The seed '**can not**' be covered! Sow five or six seeds per 15 cm (6 in) pot and place under light in a very warm place 20–25° C (68–77° F). Water from the bottom, never allowing the top of the soil to dry out.

In 6 to 8 weeks they should have sprouted enough so you can start seeing the small plants. The seeds are so small that it is hard to get only a few in each pot. If you over plant do not worry. When they get to be about 1–2 cm (.4–.8 in) tall, simply insert a pair of tweezers into the soil, about a centimetre (.4 in) deep, with one tip on either side of the seedling, close and pull. You can then take this little plug of soil and seedling and transplant it into another pot. It will

take the seedlings about four months to get to this transplantable size.

Once the seedlings are up (about 2 cm/.8 in. tall), you can water from the top. The soil must be kept moist but not too wet.

Once established, Lisianthus will flower twice a year: December/January/February and again in June/ July/ August. Of course, this depends on when you initially started them. They can do this as the new plants are coming from an established root system. If everything is to their liking, they will get up to eight buds per stem. If things are not right for them, only one of the buds will flower and the rest

Codonopsis
(Ken Pei)

will just dry up before opening. Soil that is always moist is the answer, but not wet for long periods of time. My soil is a good draining soil, high in humus. They get watered every other day here. I only fertilize twice a year, using water soluble fertilizer just before the first florets are going to open.

Wait till the plant stem is fully dead before harvesting seeds. By this time the root system should have started sending up a new stem or even multiple stems. So once the seed is harvested just cut the old stem off. The flowering stem has acted like a biennial, but has grown new offsets from its root system which are still all connected by the original root. If you are not interested in collecting the seeds (when the pods start splitting open), do not cut the old stem off until it has died on its own. If you cut it back, the root system will not have time to be able to draw nutrients from the old stem in order to produce new shoots.

I've had many Lisianthus grow for up to five years. Depending on what is flowering I cross pollinate almost every flower. I'm seeing quite a mix in flower colour and design in the ones started from my seed, from singles, to semi doubles and full doubles, from straight colours to bi-colours and even various coloured florets on one stem. The one thing a person has to be careful about is using the florets that are white as parents. White is the dominant colour when crossing with the various colours of Lisianthus. Without due diligence your Lisianthus could all eventually end up being white.

You have to be a very patient person to grow Lisianthus—I think it is a plant that is well worth the effort. They do better if planted out for the summer, rather than being left in pots, then re-pot come fall and take them in before the first frost. Planting them out in summer seems to make them a much healthier plant.

Meconopsis
Himalayan blue poppy
The blue poppy is another surprising plant that is perfectly hardy down to zone 1!

Start by planting the seed on the planting medium's surface, then, provide it with next to total darkness. Keep the soil just moist while holding the pots at temperatures of 15–18° C (59–64° F). I start them in my greenhouse by sprinkling a few seeds on the soil surface in 8 cm (3.5 in) pots. Next, place an inverted 9 cm (4 in) pot over them. Once the seeds germinate they have to be exposed to light fairly quickly (a day or two at the most). If you fail to do this, the seedlings will simply collapse. I start the seeds in late March and plant them out after the last expected spring frost, June 12th. Like Lisianthus, this plant likes a constantly moist soil, but never too wet for any length of time. It also needs a high humus soil and prefers an acidic base but will tolerate an alkaline based soil.

Meconopsis need to be planted in dappled shade – they can handle the cool morning sun, but by 11 a.m. they should have shade. The second year after being planted out the plant will flower. If things are to their liking they will even self seed in my zone 1 gardens. However once it flowers it dies, thus in this situation it acts as a biennial.

I'm not sure if one would class *Meconopsis* as biennial or perennial – I suspect it's a biennial. However, as soon as a stem starts appearing from the centre of a clump of leaves, if you pinch it out (instead of letting it flower), the plant will generate two or three offsets throughout the summer. The offsets will be individual plants the following year and the original plant will also come back – now it's acting like a form of perennial. Each of these newly grown offsets will want to send up a stem and flower next year. You now have three or four plants in a clump and can allow half of them to flower, but pinch off the stems of the other ones. Thus your patch of *Meconopsis* can be readily increased. You can have this beautiful blue Himalayan poppy or any one of the other *Meconopsis* varieties flowering in your gardens for years to come.

Codonopsis
Another Himalayan native
Also known as the skunk plant, because of the odour it can give off if damaged or rigorously disturbed.

There are many varieties belonging to this perennial family, and I haven't found one that isn't hardy down to zone 1. They are down-facing and out-facing, bell shaped florets ranging in colour from pink, white, green, red, brown and various shades of blue (from light blue to a deep purple violet). Some simply are standalones reaching about a metre in height. Other varieties are climbers and can reach two metres (6 feet) in height, while some can climb over three metres (10 feet) tall.

They will do well in dappled shade but even better in full sun so long as the soil they grow in does not get too hot from direct sunlight. Thus the soil needs shading; pansies are an excellent shade companion plant for the climbers. The pansies will come back year after year if left to self seed and at the same time provide an early spring splash of colour.

Those that are not climbers, can be planted amongst other flowers that will then provide the needed soil shade. The soil for all the various varieties of *Codonopsis* needs to be kept moist but not too wet through out the growing season.

Codonopsis are easy to start from seed: just sprinkle the seed on your planting medium's surface and keep it moist. I start the seed in late March and plant out after our last expected spring frost. They will flower in their second year and continue to become a more robust plant year after year. They will even self seed in my zone 1! 🌿

See page 111 for photos.

Problems and Solutions for Pine and Cedar Trees and Shrubs on The Prairies

by Michael Allen

Michael Allen is a Consulting Urban and Environmental Forester and Certified Arborist, Viburnum Tree Experts.

Scots pine with severe blight

Coniferous evergreens experience many problems growing in Prairie soils to which they are not native. The last couple of years have been problems for common coniferous evergreen tree and shrub varieties of pine and cedar.

Pines

Many people have called me about excessive browning of needles and what they believe to be excessive dropping of those needles from their pine trees, especially Scots pine. Their observations are correct, as both Scots pine (*Pinus sylvestris*) and Mugho pine (*Pinus mugo*) have incurred higher than normal needle losses over the last few years. Closer observation of this pine needle drop will reveal the problem lies on the twigs from

where the needles are dropping.

During the summer the green needles started to turn yellowish green and then to a straw yellow colour. Ultimately the needles turn a tan brown colour before they drop. Often the discoloured needles are in the same area as green healthy appearing needles. On closer examination the tips of the twigs are usually slightly curled or may be very prominently curled. The needles closest to the tips are either a straw brown in colour or have fallen off. Needles in the lower parts of the crown of pine trees and the lower areas of Mugho pine shrubs are affected first. The disease then moves upwards through the trees and shrubs. What is causing this twig curl, needle discolouration and needle drop? The culprit is a systemic fungus disease called pine **Sirococcus shoot blight**.

The standard treatment for this disease is to spray copper sulfate fungicide on the pine trees or shrubs in the late spring and early summer. Normally two spray treatments spaced 10 to 14 days apart are necessary. For severe disease infections a third spray might be necessary. Reapply if there is any rain within 24 hours of spraying. Generally a minimum of two continuous years of treatment are necessary. The pines should be assessed in the late summer of the second year of treatment to determine the degree of success the treatments are having.

Mugho pines can be sprayed with a dormant lime sulfur fungicide on the foliage in April or early May but before any buds open up. This fungicide is toxic to newly emerging pine shoots. A professional spray applicator should be hired to spray large trees. For smaller pine trees and shrubs the actual spraying can be done fairly easily by homeowners.

There are alternative pine species for the Prairies that seem to do reasonably well on heavier soils: ponderosa pine (*Pinus ponderosa*) and Swiss stone pine (*Pinus cembra*). Lodgepole pine (*Pinus contorta* var. *latifolia*) which is native to the foothills of Alberta and in parts of northern Alberta does not do too well on Prairie clays. It succumbs to pine needle blight and other diseases. Other Manitoba pines such as Jack pine (*Pinus banksiana*), red pine (*Pinus resinosa*) and white pine (*Pinus strobus*) do very poorly when planted on Prairie clay soils.

Cedars (Or Arborvitae)

Native eastern white cedar and many varieties of globe and columnar cedars are infested with **Fletcher scale** insects. The scale insects are present if there are clear droplets of sticky liquid (honey dew) on the leaves in late spring and summer. The newly hatched, very tiny scale nymphs or crawlers (pale yellow to light chestnut brown in colour) emerge from tiny brown spheres (adult females) in early May through to early June. Their presence can be confirmed if you wrap sticky tape sticky side up around a portion of the leaves and the twiglets.

These crawlers can be knocked off the leaves and twigs with a concentrated jet of water from a garden hose or power washer simply using water. Dormant oil can be sprayed on the leaves after the heavy frost period in early spring but before the opening of the buds. This period is usually in April, but it can vary from year to year. Reapply if there is any rain within 24 hours of spraying. Lime sulfur spray can be applied to the foliage after spraying dormant oil in April. Usually, the two dormant spray products are mixed together and sprayed at the same time.

Heavy infestation of scales can be treated later in the growing season with insecticidal soap sprays such as Safer's. Safer's soap should be applied each week for four weeks ideally starting in mid-May. Do not spray if there is any prediction of rain within 24 hours. Another series of Safer's Soap treatments may be necessary in late June to early July. Often the honey dew becomes infected with sooty mold disease leaving a greasy, blackish-green cast to the leaves.

The leaves will die if the mold infection is severe enough. When the scales are controlled, the mold is no longer a problem.

Spruce spider mites are tiny pests that suck the sap from leaves and twiglets leaving stippled dull yellowish green, tan and pale grey colours. Very fine webbing can sometimes be seen as small dense mats; if left untreated, the leaves eventually die.

This pest can be controlled with dormant oil spray in mid to late April in the same way that Fletcher scales are controlled. Hosing the cedars down with water (jet setting on the nozzle) each month from May to September will help control spider mites. Usually 5 to 6 generations of spider mites are produced during one growing season. The water pressure can physically knock off the female spider mites causing them to fall to the ground. As these females can not fly they can no longer go back into the cedars and produce new populations of spider mites.

Eastern white-cedar (*Thuja occidentalis*) which is native to Manitoba does well when planted on clay Prairie soils. Certain cultivated varieties (such as Siberian cedar and Techny cedar) of the native cedar also thrive better than other varieties on heavy clay soils. 🌿

See page 111 for photos.

Enjoy Edible Flowers:

The same colours that flowers bring to your garden can be enjoyed at the table if you open your kitchen to edible flowers. Not all flowers are edible, but those listed below can be used as garnishes or palate-pleasing ingredients.

Basil, Bee balm, Calendula petals, Chives, Daylilies, Dianthus petal tips, Lavendar, Nasturtiums, Pansies, Roses (grown without pesticides), Sage (Herb type), Scented geraniums, Signet marigold, Squash blossoms, Sunflowers,. Tuberous begonias, Tulips, Violets.

Note of caution - it is better to grow your own edible flowers because flowers raised for the florist trade often contain toxic pesticide residues.

Hellebores
Pushing The Envelope And Raising The Bar

by Sandy Venton

Sandy lives in Winnipeg, MB and has been gardening for over 50 years. Martagon lilies are her passion. She is the secretary of the North American Lily Society and the Manitoba Regional Lily Society, a lily judge, and is studying to be a Master Gardener. She lives to garden.

Hellebore in early bloom (Valerie Denesiuk)

Hellebores are not commonly found in prairie gardens. At one time they were almost never found in prairie gardens, and were never offered for sale at the local nurseries. I saw my first one here in Winnipeg at St. Mary's Nursery a number of years ago and immediately purchased it, hang the expense!

I met my first Hellebore when I lived in Vancouver, BC. There were Hellebores all over the place, mostly *Helleborus niger*, more commonly known as 'the Christmas rose', which opens very early in midwinter and stays green all year. The flowers are generally a white/cream colour, also pale pink. *Helleborus orientalis*, now known as *Helleborus* x *hybridus*, the Lenten rose, opens around Easter, also stays green all year and flowers in varying shades ranging from pale pink to almost black. I use the term 'shade' for two reasons. First of all, because rather than tints, which add white to the colours on the colour wheel, shades add black to the aforesaid colours, and secondly because Hellebores grow best in a shaded location. *Helleborus* is a small genus in the family *Ranunculaceae*, and as such, all parts of the plant are poisonous.

There are a great number of species of Hellebores, however, the two mentioned above are the ones most commonly offered by nurseries. That being said, just because you go out and purchase a Hellebore, there is no guarantee that it will either like its new location, or that it will survive. Now, in my considered opinion, any fool can grow things in Vancouver, but it takes a dedicated gardener to get things to grow on the prairies in general, and in Manitoba in particular. And that goes in spades regarding Hellebores.

They prefer a semi-shady damp spot in the garden, and I discovered that when I planted my first Hellebore under a spruce tree near the house, thinking that it would get winter protection and a fairly acid soil. Huh! That Hellebore came up for a few years, didn't flower, and then when it finally did flower, it sent up one trembly stem with one flower.

The Hellebore languished in that spot for a few more years, and then simply gave up the ghost. But not being one to give up and lie down, I purchased another Hellebore from one of my favourite nurseries in Salt Spring Island, BC that carries hard-to-find perennials that may or may not survive our Winnipeg winters. The new Hellebore was planted in a different spot, on the north side of our garage, in a north-facing bed, no trees, late to thaw, and which remains fairly damp all summer. That proved to be the answer and the next spring the Hellebores came up, flowered, and flourished. That being said, I have since read that Hellebores can take full sun, provided that adequate moisture is provided. As well, some Hellebore species thrive in a more alkaline soil. So nothing about growing Hellebores is cut and dried. When you consider that some of the hybrids offered for sale have several different species in their genetic

makeup, all bets are off, and all you can do is place them in a nice, well-drained spot, with adequate moisture, plenty of organic matter and hope for the best.

I am sad to report that the old garage will be torn down this coming summer, and all plants in that particular shade bed, which was my pride and joy and the apple of my eye, must be dismantled, dug up and the plants placed in pots until the new garage will be built and a new shade bed prepared.

On the basis of good luck rather than good gardening with that particular new Hellebore site, and prior to the arrangements for a new garage being made, I ordered several more Hellebores. While the first ones were red, the new ones will be "blue" (more of a purple-blue), "black" (more of a very dark purple) and several pink selections. Doubles will follow in the future, hopefully. I am keeping all fingers crossed that they do as well in the new spot as did the ones in the old location. It just figures, though, that just when I found the perfect spot for them, they have to be dug up. Of course, most books on the particular subject say that Hellebores dislike being disturbed. I will have to be very careful and dig up as much surrounding soil with the plant as possible, as what struck me while reading about them, was the instruction that "Hellebores must never be dug up using a trowel."

Which brings me back to both colour and shape. *Helleborus* x *hybridus* are now offered in varying shades of white, cream, pale pink, rosy pink, rosy red, indigo, purple, yellow, and pale colours with varying colored spots. There are also double cultivars being offered, but until the prices are lowered somewhat, my Zone 2B (formerly 3A) garden will have to plod along without them. It's one thing to spend money on a plant that may or may not survive, but it's sheer folly to spend a fortune on a plant without making absolutely sure that it will make it through its first Manitoba winter. It all depends on snow cover, and while this past winter my gardens were more than adequately covered by the "white mulch", there is no guarantee that future winters will behave the same way. Proper mulching would be advised, rather than relying on heavy snowfalls.

Hellebores are neither showy, like roses or peonies or irises, nor are they bright and cheery, like daffodils and crocuses and tulips, however, they do have a shy and subtle charm of their own. While most cup-shaped flowers raise their heads gladly towards the sun, the Hellebores, probably because they open so very early in the spring – practically as soon as the snow disappears – keep their heads facing downwards so as not to get buffeted by late winter/ early spring storms. Which makes me all the more glad to see them when they do arrive!

Hellebores were named Plant of the Year in 2005, and because of that, they went from relative obscurity to all-out popularity. That is all very well and good for those lucky souls who live in Zone 4 and up. But for us hardy folk living on the Canadian Prairies, which can be the most inhospitable and changeable climate on earth, growing Hellebores is not a snap, but a labour of love. It's worth it to stand there and look at a flower that probably has no business blooming in a Winnipeg garden, but isn't prairie gardening all about pushing the envelope to the very edge? And beyond? 🌿

See page 112 for photos.

Start Gardening with Beans

Bush beans or pole beans are easy to grow and fun for children to watch turn into dinner. Wait till soil temperature is warm. Space seeds four to six inches apart, placing the eyes down. Plant some again in two weeks for a longer supply. Beans grow best in full sunshine with regular moisture. Pick when beans are about ¼ inch in diameter before the beans swell in the pods. Do not walk among your beans when wet with rain or dew.

The Gardens of the Commonwealth War Graves Commission

by Warren Otto

Warren Otto is Program Administrator, Prairie Horticulture Certificate at the University of Manitoba, and the Maple Leaf Legacy Project Regional Representative for Manitoba and Northwest Ontario.

In April 2007 volunteers of the Maple Leaf Legacy Project (www.mapleleaflegacy.org) met in France to tour the Western Front and cemeteries of the Commonwealth War Graves Commission.

The Commission, founded by Sir Fabian Ware, had its beginnings as the Graves Registration Commission in 1915, before the Imperial (later Commonwealth) War Graves Commission was established by Royal Charter on May 21, 1917. From its earliest beginnings, Ware encouraged help from distinguished horticulturists at the Royal Botanic Gardens at Kew, and famous architects of the day, on how cemeteries should be designed. Burial grounds along the Western Front were designed to be less bleak, by growing annual and perennial flowers, grass, shrubs and trees. The concept created a sentimental association between the gardens of home and the foreign fields where soldiers lie. The Commission continues this tradition by planting species native to its member countries in cemeteries

wherever possible. The horticultural design of each cemetery is to give the effect of a garden, where the harmonious combination of the various elements may help the visitor achieve a sense of peace in a beautiful and serene setting.

Front borders of each headstone are 45-60 cm wide and planted with low growing herbaceous plants so as to not obscure engraved personal inscriptions. The plants also prevent soil from splashing on headstones during rain. Plants between headstones are taller. A typical border scheme is made up of approximately twenty plant species, providing variety of texture, height and timing of floral display. Certain rows have a floral border behind the headstones, adding a further dimension to the plantings. Dwarf and low growing shrubs, herbaceous perennials, grasses and ground covering plants are chosen to extend the floral display.

Where a sufficient water supply is available, lawns are used in cemeteries throughout the world. The lawns

Beny-sur-Mer Canadian War Cemetery, France

provide the appropriate setting for the borders, and the absence of paths contributes to the cemetery design. The use of trees, shrubberies, hedges and sometimes pergolas contribute to the architectural layout of a cemetery. These features also help give interest, form and coherence to the design, while providing shelter, obscuring unwanted sights and defining borders.

Pedestal grave markers used in countries, such as Thailand and Turkey, require a different kind of floral border. Plants are dwarf in harmony with the low pedestals and arranged in specific scheme, similar to headstone borders.

Since the Commission strives to use lawn wherever possible, irrigation is used where natural rainfall is insufficient. The irrigation systems are computer controlled which allows for water to be provided during the night, reducing evaporation and minimising waste. In places where irrigation is impractical, such as Gallipoli, seed mixtures of drought tolerant grasses are used to provide resilience during the long dry summer months. There are certain cemeteries, such as El Alamein in Egypt and Tobruk in Libya, where the natural desert landscape invite a different approach to planting. There are no lawns and plants are selected for their drought tolerance. In Rhodes War Cemetery, Greece, pebbles are used instead of grass and the colourful borders are set in these, producing a different result, reflecting the dry local landscape.

The total ground area within the Commission's control is approximately 710ha, of which over 450ha are under fine horticultural maintenance.

Since maintaining the cemeteries to the Commission's exacting standards is very labour intensive, the Commission employs approximately nine hundred gardeners throughout the world. In many cases children and grandchildren of former gardeners carry on the family tradition by working for the Commission. War graves within civil cemeteries are typically maintained under contract with the local authority or landscape contractor.

Throughout the growing season, gardeners are involved in ceaseless rounds of mowing, hoeing, edging, scarification, pruning and deadheading. During the dormant season cultivating and replanting the headstone borders and re-levelling and resowing turf take over. Hedges, shrubberies and trees are also planted during the dormant season.

Since first experimenting with lawn mowers in 1920, the Commission has continued to adopt new technology, helping to lighten the gardener's load. Compact tractors, stump grinders, wood chippers, edge trimmers, leaf blowers and collectors, scarifiers, aerators, over-seeders and rotovators are now common equipment of the Commission gardeners. Gardeners are supported by technical supervisory staff and a Director of Horticulture in the maintenance of more than 2500 war cemeteries, plots and grounds throughout the world.

Thanks to Sir Fabian Ware's vision and the dedication of the current staff, the names of Commonwealth war dead will live on forever, telling the true story of the horrors of war. 🐾

Acidifying Garden Soils
by Ieuan Evans

Dr Evans is a well know plant pathologist with vast agronomic expertise who lives in Spruce Grove, AB

Generally speaking, most garden ornamental and crop plants grow best at a pH of 6 to 7, i.e. soil that is slightly on the acid side. The pH scale, which is a measure of hydrogen ion concentration, ranges from 0, which is an extremely corrosive acid to 14, an extremely alkaline base. Concentrated hydrochloric acid would be a 0 and concentrated caustic soda would be a 14. When both combine to form common table salt the pH of these ions Na (sodium) and Cl (chloride) becomes a neutral 7.

On the Canadian prairies from Ontario to British Columbia our soil pH might range from 3 to a high of 10 or more. Most of the British Colombia soils are acidic as are those of Western Ontario. In the three Prairie Provinces, around 30% of Alberta's agricultural soils can be classified as acidic with pHs below 6 whereas only 10% of Saskatchewan's and 5% of Manitoba's soils fall into this category. Soils in the Northern non-agricultural shield areas of all three provinces are acidic often with pH values of 4.5 and lower.

Crop and ornamental plant species can be either tolerant of a range of soil pH values or sometimes very sensitive to either high or low pH soil values, i.e. basic or acidic soils. Many garden ornamentals and crop plants will grow well from pH 5.5 to 8.5 whereas many plant species will only thrive if the pH is preferably less than 5.0 or above 6 or 6.5. They may classify plants that prefer high pH soils as **calcecole** and those that prefer low pH as **calcifuges**. In parts of the prairies where the soil pH changes significantly, say from pH 7 to pH 5, so do the native plant species that are present. Blueberries and their relatives will not grow in soils with a pH above 6. They only grow best in soils that range from 3.5 to 5. So when you see large tracts of blueberry bushes in Canada, you are looking at acidic soils, common on the Northern prairies and in Ontario and British Columbia. Such soils are often unsuitable for most agricultural crops, unless they are limed. Carrots, cauliflower, potatoes and tomatoes will grow well in soils that range in pH 5.5 to 7.5. Soil pHs from 8 to 9 are not uncommon on the southern prairies – many crop and ornamental plants will grow, but they do not perform very well. Crops such as lettuce, basil and onions, and flowers like lilies, begonias and petunias are at their best in acidic soils.

So what's happening in high or low pH soils that either causes plants to die out or not perform very well? At soils with pHs below 5, for example, wheat plants will take up toxic amounts of soluble aluminum. At soil pHs of 5.5 and up, this very common soil mineral is insoluble and unavailable for uptake by the wheat crop. At a soil pH below 6, alfalfa plants cannot fix nitrogen since the symbiotic rhizobial bacteria necessary for this process do not survive in acidic soils. In addition, an essential mineral such as molybdenum involved in the nitrogen fixing process becomes insoluble and unavailable in the acidic soil. When the soil pH moves above 7, most essential plant micronutrients are less available to growing plants. At a soil pH of 8 or higher the micronutrients such as copper, iron, manganese and zinc become 10 times less available, i.e. insoluble or very poorly available. I'm sure many of you have seen the iron induced chlorosis that causes a bright yellowing of the leaves of trees and shrubs that occurs in high pH soils, generally soils with a pH of 8 or 8.5. This iron induced chlorosis occurs at this high pH despite the fact that most soils are from 2–10% by weight made up of iron compounds. In other words, there are huge amounts of iron in most soils, but very high pH makes the iron unavailable to growing plants. By no means do we fully understand the role of soil pH in plant growth, but we are beginning to understand some of the chemical, biochemical and biological mechanisms.

We know that in many parts of Europe there are acidic soils and that it was lime (limestone) or dolomitic lime (calcium and magnesium) that was essential for improved crop production. The lime was necessary to raise the pH often from 3.5 to around a pH of 6. This raise in pH needed several tons of lime per crop acre. This is still commonly done in British Columbia and Eastern Canada. On the farm that I grew up on in Wales, the land was 'limed' every 10 to 15 years in order to increase crop productivity. Excepting Alberta, the only need for lime on the prairies in most areas is as a top dressing for lawns that are 15 to 30 years old. This is due to the fact that frequent fertilizer and watering along with a build-up of thatch will turn the top 5–15 cm (2–6 in) acidic. The acidic lawn results in a decline of the alkaliloving bluegrasses and an invasion of weeds such as dandelions.

How do you modify alkali soils so that ornamental and crop plants grow to the best of their abilities? If, for example, you have a garden soil pH of around 7.5 to 9 there is nothing that you can do practically to immediately lower the soil pH. If you are moving into a new house in any of our major cities that invariably has alkaline soil or subsoil, you could import acidic topsoil for the top 10–20 cm (4–8 in) of your new garden. Acidic topsoil particularly available in

Alberta is from 4.5 to 6.5. Practically the only way to significantly lower the pH of the soil in your garden is by the addition of elemental sulphur. Elemental sulphur commonly used in prairie agriculture can be purchased by the bag from major fertilizer dealers. This sulphur in the form of small pellets is a byproduct of the oil and gas industry and is considered to be an 'organic' nutrient.

When the pelleted elemental sulphur is applied to garden soil the pellets breakdown on contact with soil moisture into a fine dust or powder. In the soil primarily *thiobaccilus* bacteria will convert this elemental sulphur in an oxidation process that supplies energy – sulphuric acid. In dry, low fertility soils, low in organic matter, this process of conversion could take up to 5 years or more. In moist, well-maintained soil the conversion process may only be a couple of years. The sulphuric acid produced will convert alkali calcium or magnesium carbonate to the neutral calcium or magnesium sulphate form. It takes 14½ kg (32 lb) of

sulphur to neutralize 45 kg (100 lb) of limestone (calcium carbonate). A high pH soil with 'free lime' at the 1% level contains 105 kg (230 lb) of calcium carbonate in 93 square m (1,000 square ft) of soil, therefore, it would require 33½ kg (74 lb) of sulphur to be converted to neutral calcium sulphate.

For very small areas of the garden, say 9½ square m (100 square ft), use one tenth of the above rates for sensitive acid loving species such as azaleas, rhododendrons or blueberries. To change such soils to these lowered rates will take anything from 2 to 5 years to materialize. In plant pots or small containers the soil pH can be lowered quickly by either using a soilless plant mix with added peat moss or by watering with aluminum sulphate. The aluminum sulphate can change soil pHs rapidly especially on soilless mixes but it is not economical to use on a garden scale. Aluminum sulphate would be used for the few isolated plants in the garden if immediate action is required, say for a failing azalea or rhododendron. One

Practical Sulphur Application Rules				
Pelleted elemental sulphur should be well worked in pounds per 1,000 square feet of garden at the following rates:				
Existing pH	Desired pH	Clay	Loam	Sandy loam
8	7.0	32	20	8
	6.5	47	29	12
7.5	7.0	16	10	4
	6.5	32	20	8
7.0	6.5	16	10	4
	6.0	32	20	8

of the myths that persist in Alberta is that spruce or pine trees in your garden will make the soil acidic. Pine or spruce trees will no more alter your garden soil pH than any deciduous tree or shrub.

Aluminum sulphate for acidifying small quantities of soil or soil for pot plants, can be obtained in most box stores or horticultural outlets in 2 kg (4½ lb) containers. One manufacturer is Nu-Gro IP Inc. Brantford, Ontario.(www.cil.nu-gro.com). Sulphur is only available on a farm scale which can be purchased at any farm fertilizer dealer at around 40- 50 cents a pound. You will likely have to buy a 22½ kg (50 lb) bag unless you can persuade the dealer to sell smaller amounts. One of the major suppliers is Tigersul products, Calgary (Tigersul.com). Their product Tiger 90CR is a granular that emulsifies on contact with the soil. If you need to apply a pound of this product, then you apply 1.1 lbs. since it is only 90% sulphur. Remember, when you acidify alkaline soil with sulphur, you not only lower the soil pH, but you release soil phosphate, reduce soil crusting, allow better water penetration, remove sodium and allow for better soil aeration. Elemental sulphur is considered by many organic organisations to be an organic product. 🦫

To Demystify the Alpine
by Amanda Botincan

Amanda (Mandy) Botincan is the owner/operator of Mandy's Greenhouses near Tyndall, Manitoba (www.mandysgreenhouse.com). She grows many fruit trees, grapes, raspberries, roses, a large vegetable garden and at one time, numerous huge perennials, now replaced with every conceivable alpine/rock garden plant she can lay her hands.

Historical records show rock gardens originating in the British Isles. Early travellers of the 19th Century venturing over to Switzerland and other mountainous European regions were awed by the spectacular and unusual plant material they saw en route. Never having seen these plants in their homeland, some were inspired to return with 'just a few' in an attempt to grow them at home.

The Victorian Era was famous for its Rockeries, bearing no resemblance to alpine/rock gardens of today. The focus leaned more toward architectural grottos, arches, bridges and other hardscape elements, leav-

ing the flower garden to become a
graveyard for the newly transplanted
choice alpines transported from
their original homes. The majority
of plants brought back were totally
foreign to this new environment.
Information on how to grow them
was nowhere to be found, either
by word of mouth or from books.
Occasionally, some hardy sorts
survived, lucky to have been placed
into similar growing conditions, or
because they were able to adapt.

Eventually, alpines managed
to flourish. The Europeans seemed
to learn how to tend them ahead
of everyone else. In the early 1800s
and later that century, the British
began to grow alpines, successfully,
in earnest. In 1870 William Robinson wrote a book called *Alpine
Flowers for the English Garden*. With
his guidance the skills of local rock
gardeners began to improve. Despite
more alpine writer experts such as
Reginald Farrer, Lewis Meredith and
Henri Correvon, many alpines were
lost to the cause of Rock Gardening.

North Americans joined the
challenge in the 1920s, attempting
to construct copies of the famous
Kew Botanical Garden of England
<www.kew.org>, including its rock
gardens, in 1920 and 1932. Soon
after, in 1934, the North American
Rock Garden Society (NARGS)
<www.narg.org> was founded. This
society now has 4,500 members.
It was and is still one of the best
architects of exhibits; hosts of alpine

flower shows and garden visits;
sources of superb photography,
excellent informative newsletters
and quarterly publications; and
holds one of the largest alpine seed
exchanges in the world.

Today alpine enthusiasts are making tremendous inroads in seeking
out charming plants from all over the
world to grace our alpine and rock gardens. North American gardeners have
acquired extensive knowledge in the
management and requirements of alpines. We are now able to place almost
any choice plant into an environment
designed to be so close to the plant's
original setting that it feels it never left,
which is the way it should be.

An alpine is defined by its ability to survive some of the harshest
environments nature has to offer.
Some of the most desirable specimens can be found growing above
the tree line at elevations higher
than one would care to climb.

Imagine if you can ... a *Lewisia
rediviva* (Bitterroot) dangling at a
45° angle on the edge of a mountain
slope or hilly peak beside a bonsai
pine, thinking nothing of the view or
the sharp drop! How about a clump
of *Primula japonica* (Japanese Primrose) or the famous English wildflower *Primula veris* (English Cowslip)
dipping their feet in moist peaty bogs
along a woodland edge? And in the
distance, a drift of yellow *Hymenoxys
acaulis* (Angelita Daisy), straight
ahead *Penstemon fruticosus* (Lowbush
Penstemon), and tucked just out of

sight behind a blind of granite the elusive *Castilleja rhexifolia* (Alpine Paintbrush), tossing their heads to and fro in the shifting winds of the vast meadows and valleys. Several hundred miles away, in a desert plain, is the perfect home for *Sedum stenopetalum* (Wormleaf Stonecrop), *Astragalus purshii* (Woollypod Milkvetch) and *Lomatium grayi* (Biscuitroot) ... a species preferring dry, rainless summers. Alpines ... all of them, each thriving in its own unique habitat. Extreme moisture fluctuations, wide temperature ranges, low nutrient levels, grazing cattle, short growing seasons and harsh winds are all qualities that the 'true alpine' takes in stride with grace and perseverance.

Some alpines are not all that particular about the soil in which they grow. For instance, I have a *Silene acaulis* (Moss Campion), a choice ground creeper, that has thrived in sticky Red River gumbo for the past 5 years. However, preferred mediums are sand, gravel, rock chips, peat and yes, chalky clay. All are palatable, providing that the medium is lean in nutrition and drains well. The key to survival for an alpine is to NEVER allow it to have wet feet, except the bog-lovers, of course. For air hungry alpines, if water engulfs their roots for more than a day, death will surely follow by oxygen starvation.

As creatures of habit and adaptation, alpines will do almost anything to survive. To accommo-date their habitat, they will reduce their size (tighter to the ground) and adjust their shape to minimize exposure to harsh winds. Spiny, leafy mounds are definitely less attractive to grazing wild animals. Some go dormant in summer, while others vacation in winter. Thicker leathery or grass-like micro-sized leaves aid the tiny plants in their bid to stay alive. Hairy leaves are special – keeping the tissues warm and collecting condensation when rains fail to show. Long, extensive root systems provide a dual purpose: to look for nutrients and to assist in clinging onto rough inhospitable surfaces. And the flowers—oh, the flowers! They are colourful: intense yellows, blues, reds, whites, oranges, blacks and purples; prolific and huge in comparison to the rest of the plant. They come in all shapes and sizes. Seasons are short. Bright, beautiful, large flowers attract the proper pollinating insects, ensuring a better quantity of seed for the future.

The true alpine is indeed a contender for the 'Survival of the Fittest and Lets have a Party While We're At It' award. To know and grow alpines is to appreciate and respect nature at its finest. I encourage you to try a few yourself! Let's see if you can stop at one or two? ❧

See page 112 for photos.

"Fast Plant Nation"
by Colleen Zacharias

Colleen is an avid container gardener, president of the Friends of the Conservatory and The Prairie Garden co-chair. She lives in Winnipeg, MB

The critically acclaimed book, "Fast Food Nation", written by Eric Schlosser and published by Houghton Mifflin Books in 2001 became a successful movie in 2006. The book's subtitle is "The Dark Side of the All-American Meal" and focuses on the phenomenal impact of fast food on the food industry and its role in popular culture.

Fast food, while not always satisfying, is at least convenient and meets the needs of a hectic lifestyle. Are we also becoming a 'fast plant nation'? Do our busy schedules leave little time for the careful nurturing and coaxing that many plants require? Just as the term 'slow food' evokes a vision of a carefully prepared meal consisting of local ingredients purchased at the neighborhood farmer's market, a 'slow plant' is more likely one that is native to one's growing region. Native growing conditions do not guarantee perfect plants. Often they must be painstakingly cared for until, finally, sometimes after a few seasons, the gardener is rewarded with the desired results.

An appetite demanding instant gratification may have little patience for the effort that may be required to produce a single, perfect bloom. It is far easier to place a 'super size' order and should the plant's performance prove lackluster, it can easily be replaced with another. While that approach may be a different take on the art of gardening, it also eliminates the need to select zone-hardy plants or to match a particular plant to specific growing conditions. It would also allow for more leisure time in the late fall. Certainly there would be no need for mulching if the plant is only taking up temporary space!

The tempting array of plants available at garden centers includes many exotic plants that would survive a prairie winter only in the safe confines of an indoor micro-climate. The 'wow' factor, though, when luscious zone 5 or 6 plants show off their blooms in the garden or in a container is not to be denied. Many gardeners will carefully transplant their non-zone-hardy plants to the indoors at the first nip in the fall air. There is another breed of gardeners, though, who will simply dispose of the plants, rationalizing that the dramatic single-season display justifies the extra expense of purchasing new plants next season. This is not without benefit to the local greenhouse.

Undoubtedly, there is tremendous satisfaction in seeing a long-loved and cared for plant make its appearance once again in the spring and feel sorrow if it does not. Gardening is presumed to be a leisure activity and hardly seems synonymous with a lack of time to nurture. Still, there is a growing trend that is likely to put its own unique stamp on this time-honored tradition. From satisfying the demand for the latest *plant du jour*, with zone hardiness as a secondary concern,

to creating an instant, lush oasis where poor performers are ousted quickly, a revolutionary approach to gardening is finding its niche in the marketplace.

While the idea of disposable plants may seem like heresy to the traditional gardener, the temporary plant can always be disposed of in the compost bin so as to nourish the soil for tomorrow's plants. 🐦

---

50 Years Ago – The New African Violet
by A. W. Sellers

This article was originally printed in the 1960 Prairie Garden

There has been a remarkable improvement in the African Violet in recent years. Each year there are new innovations brought forth. Attendance at any African Violet show is a treat for the African Violet lover, but the international African Violet Convention held in the United States each spring is a spectacle that is breath-taking. It consists of large commercial exhibits of exhibitors creations, their new seedlings and other well grown specimens made up into an artistic exhibit. Included is an amateur show of exhibits entered by members of the Society. These plants are grown for exhibition purposes and have been grown with great care and attention. The scientist, the professional hybridizer and the hobbyist hybridizer meet here on common ground, all with one interest, the

African Violet. There is keen interest to see what the other fellow has come up with since the last showing, and we also see to what perfection African Violets can be grown.

The scientist's ability to look into the future with their understanding of plant cells, nuclei, chromosomes and genes have worked wonders, as well as the professional hybridizer who is working to give us what we want. The men and women who hybridize the African Violet as a hobby also have produced many of the most sought after plants each year. African Violets are easily multiplied and so this new material is available to all to work with in new lines.

Mutations come about naturally, but also can be induced artificially. It is from these "breaks" that the present day African Violet has come.

There are types that reproduce reasonably true to form. One, designated "Supreme" is an extra large plant whose leaves are inclined to be coarse. It has a full range of variations in foliage with single and double flowers. It is the ideal type to be put on a table by itself near a window getting the owner's personal attention. A mature plant is at home in a four inch pot.

Then, we have the medium-sized plant, by far the most popular and greatest in number. Its place is on the window sill or an arrangement in color combinations as table or room decorations. it lends itself to artistic grouping. They are the preferred show type. Three inches is the maximum size pot recommended by most experienced growers.

The miniatures have a dwarf appearance but can be grown to perfection in symmetry of foliage with single and double flowers in good range of form and colour. When one looks at well grown plants, "Aren't they cute?" is a natural exclamation. Don't over-pot this type, two and one-half inch pots or less are desirable.

In the past, there are many flowers that have caught the fancy of the public, but as a house plant, none have reached the popularity of the African Violet of today. All old violets are not necessarily poor plants, but the tendency each year is to improvement. In talking to one of the leading hybridizers, the writer asked: "What do you do with the hundreds of plants in your crosses that aren't better than their parents?" The answer was: "We destroy them". Each year he produces one, two or three, maybe a few more that are tops. Nothing that is not better, survives. They are easy to grow if just a few are to be looked after. Every home has some spot in which several will do well. Just remember, they are living things and need some attention. If peculiarities show up, ask your local African Violet Society and they will be only too glad to share their knowledge with you.

Now, for the type you would prefer, and for convenience we will discuss the medium size as it has the greatest range of foliage and variations with color, and form of flower.

Do you prefer singles? If so, keep in mind that they do not hold their blossoms as long as the doubles. There are good single whites and colors of all shades of pink, blue, purple, wine and some very close to red. Many of the base colours have picotee edges, deep pink on light pink, white on blue or purple, lacy fringed edged petals most delicate in appearance.

One of the most recent "breaks" is a chartreuse edge green, yellow or gold in appearance depending on shade according to age of blossom. This introduction is being used extensively in this year's hybridizing, and something is sure to come of it. It is very attractive and some think it will lead to the elusive yellow.

Two of the leading hybrid-izers residing miles apart and not knowing that each were working on the same project, came up with the "Stars". The flower has a distinct "Star" appearance and is very attractive. Some of the "Stars" have very small undeveloped petals in the centre that serve the purpose of holding the blossom on the stems much longer than the true single.

As to the doubles, they have every-thing the singles have with this in addition: the blossoms stay on until the mature and dry up. The demand has been for doubles, therefore, the professional hybrid-izers has produced what we asked for. The writer has visited some of the leading commercial greenhouses specialising in African Violets. Their benches are scenes of indescribable beauty, a mass of colour that only the double violet can give in its size and profusion or blooms. The advance in the double blossom plant is in semi-double to good form of blossom, large, fully double and made up of evenly sized, overlapping petals borne on straight stiff stems holding the flowers well above the foliage. It was only a very short time ago that the great fault the prolific double bloomer had was the weight of the bloom was too heavy for the stems and they would lie down. This has been overcome.

The foliage of the original African Violet has been changed until it has been said: "It is no longer a violet". It is true, there has been a drastic change, but for the 'better. It is what violet lovers wanted and any changes found ready markets.

Leaves are divided into two types — girl and boy. They both can be classed dark, medium and light in shades of green on the surface. The underside ranges from almost white to reddish maroon.

The hybridizers have worked up some very beautiful foliage in both singles and doubles, from light fringed to heavily ruffled edges. Many exclamations of delight are heard from viewers at the beauty of the foliage before the blossom is noticed.

It may have been that you were not successful in your attempts to grow African Violets. It is being done with marvellous success giving great happiness to many people for little effort. Perhaps you didn't have the right one for your environment, or a local condition is now correct-ed. Try some of the new introduc-tions — most of the 1959 releases are available. Our importers know they have a demand for the new ones and cater to our wants. Any person interested in African Violets can grow them successfully.

San Francisco is the site of the 1962 convention. A prominent grower says they will have a selection of yellow and all green flowers on ex-hibit. We have been waiting for just that, so let us plan to see them. ❧

The 2009 Prairie Garden Award for Excellence
by Linda Pearn

The Prairie Garden Award for Excellence for 2009 was presented to two recipients – **Ken Ivey** & **Brenda Cameron** (Virden, MB) and **Albert Parsons** (Minnedosa, MB) – at a luncheon at Larters at St. Andrews on Thursday, September 3, 2009. This is the tenth year this Award has been given for Excellence in Horticulture on the Northern Great Plains. Information for the following articles has been excerpted from the nomination papers.

KEN IVEY and BRENDA CAMERON of Virden, MB

Ken and Brenda were volunteer co-chairs of Manitoba Communities in Bloom from 1999 to 2008.

The Communities in Bloom program began in 1995. Virden registered in the program beginning in 1996. Brenda Cameron co-chaired the Virden in Bloom committee and Ken Ivey was an active committee member. This was the beginning of their interest and dedication to the program which quickly caught on across the province and country. In 1999 the national office approached Ken and Brenda to create and manage a provincial office for CIB. They willingly took on this volunteer role and continued to manage the provincial program until 2008.

In their first year as provincial co-coordinators, Ken and Brenda and the Virden in Bloom committee hosted the first provincial awards and seminars event in Virden in

Ken Ivey & Brenda Cameron
(Sandy Venton)

1999. They have worked with a host community every year since doing all that is necessary to organize this annual event. These weekend events have educational speakers and opportunities for communities to network and to share best-practices. "Communities in Bloom, People, Plants and Pride… Growing Together" - that is what it is all about. It is about improving communities so that people, plants, and pride can all grow in a community and Ken and Brenda have guided communities to do just that.

During their ten years in office, 57 Manitoba communities have participated in the Communities in Bloom program and having seen the benefits, many communities have stayed with the program for many years.

Communities in Bloom judges evaluate communities based on a scoring grid made up of eight categories which are: Tidiness, Environmental awareness, Community Involvement, Heritage Conservation, Landscaped Areas, Urban Forestry, Floral Displays and Turf and Ground Cover. Each category is broken down into 4 sections to gauge the involvement and contribution of each sector of the community. The 4 sectors are municipal, commercial/industrial, residential, and groups/organizations (this includes churches, schools, sports clubs, not-for-profits, etc.)

Because of the nature of the program, by getting communities involved, positive changes have taken place in many communities and how they go about accomplishing improvements. They have encouraged new communities to become involved by traveling to communities to make presentations, attend trade shows, and through letters and newsletters. Once communities have registered, they communicate with them to give them guidance on how to get started, ways to form their committees, etc.

With all sectors of the community involved, there is also a greater capacity to fund projects. Instead of leaving things up to the municipality, businesses and citizens also contribute financial and in kind support. Memorial plantings are self funded with donations. Ken and Brenda have worked very hard to promote the goals and educational opportunities of the Communities in Bloom Program. The seminars and awards weekend have become known as great places to learn new methods and best practices, and bring together those who want to make changes to learn and share. The standard of care, particularly in horticulture, has risen dramatically. By inspiring change in communities to make them appear more attractive and welcoming, many spin off benefits occur in the areas of tourism, economic development, and attracting new residents for relocation. People feel better about where they live.

Another responsibility of Ken and Brenda in their role as co-chairs was to recruit provincial judges that were interested in the program and willing to volunteer one or two weeks of their summer to travel to communities to do evaluations and then spending several hours filling out evaluations. By sourcing highly qualified judges, Ken and Brenda have made it possible for communities to receive very valuable information when judges visit and provide written evaluations.

An additional partnership they formed was with the Composting Council. They were able to partner to secure funding to create an opportunity for communities to sell composters as a fundraiser while raising awareness of the value of composting.

CIB also makes people realize that heritage is not only buildings, costumes, etc. but that they have heritage trees, native stands of plants, etc. and they are all worth noting and preserving.

To summarize, as part of their volunteer duties in the Manitoba in Bloom office, Ken and Brenda have sourced judges, coordinated the judges tour schedule, held judges training seminars, provided communities with information about the program, and carried out the many responsibilities required to host the provincial awards weekend and looked after the day to day operations of the office.

As provincial co-chairs, Ken and Brenda were also members of the National Communities in Bloom Committee for ten years. Since they have retired from the responsibility of managing the provincial office, they continue to be involved in the MB CIB program. Ken is president of the provincial MB CIB committee and Brenda is also an active committee member. Brenda is also entering her second year as a volunteer judge for Communities in Bloom.

Along with their variety of responsibilities with the Manitoba Communities in Bloom, Ken and Brenda have continued working as part of Virden in Bloom committee.

Virden has registered as a competitor in the program, mentored new communities or participated in a networking capacity. Brenda has served as co-chair of the Virden in Bloom committee for many years.

Ken and Brenda have also both been active in their home community of Virden and in organizations in the region. Ken owned and operated Ivey Greenhouses for 20 years along with his wife Susan. They graduated from Canadian School of Floral Art in Hamilton, ON. Ken has been a member of Chamber of Commerce, Virden Wallace Economic Development Board and Wheat Belt Community Futures Board. Brenda owns and operates Virden School & Office Supplies; is involved in curling, golf and a member of the Virden Art Club. She loves to work in her flower and vegetable gardens.

Congratulations, Ken Ivey and Brenda Cameron, on winning The Prairie Garden Award for Excellence for 2009.

See the next page for the second The Prairie Garden Award for Excellence recipient.

ALBERT PARSONS
of Minnedosa, MB

Albert has been involved in horticulture since childhood when he grew house plants and helped tend the family garden. He became an educator and horticulture was a hobby, then a secondary occupation and after retirement, a second career.

Albert Parsons
with his daughter Joanne & wife Edith

Albert and his wife Edith moved to Birtle, MB in 1970, at which time he began to exhibit in horticultural shows in the area. He grew plants for his own use in his greenhouse and eventually began supplying gardeners with extras. This grew into a larger business which lasted for twelve years.

In the late 1980's, Albert began working on his Ontario Diploma in Horticulture from Guelph University, ON. He moved to Carberry, MB in 1991 and continued with his diploma training. He joined the Carberry Horticultural Society and was president for a number of years. He was involved in developing an open gardens day in Carberry and continued to share his gardening experiences with other gardeners.

After retirement from education, Albert and his wife moved to Minnedosa, MB in 1998. Here he became involved with the Minnedosa Horticultural Society and has served several terms as president. He is involved with the Minnedosa Business Development Committee's beautification program and has served on the Minnedosa Communities in Bloom committee and also as a provincial Communities in Bloom judge. Albert was chair of the Manitoba Horticultural Convention committee when the Minnedosa Horticultural Society hosted it in 2003.

In his retirement, Albert established a business called Gardens By Design through which he offers garden design advise, landscaping consultation, and offers workshops and presentations to groups on a regular basis.

Albert has also devoted more time to writing. He has published two books, *Gardening In All Four Seasons, Volumes I and II.* He has established himself as a regional horticultural writer and has been published in *The Manitoba Gardener, The Gardener for the Prairies, The Western Producer,* and *Grainews.* He continues to be a regular contributor to *The Manitoba Co-operator* and his weekly garden column still appears in *The Brandon Sun.*

Albert willingly shares his knowledge and expertise, his garden and its produce, and his love of gardening and the joy it brings him.

Congratulations, Albert Parsons, on winning The Prairie Garden Award for Excellence for 2009.

The Prairie Garden
Award for Excellence

has been presented annually since 2000 by The Prairie Garden in order to recognize horticultural achievements.

Eligibility

The Prairie Garden Award for Excellence shall be awarded to an individual or group making a significant contribution to the advancement and/or promotion of horticulture on the Northern Great Plains. Areas of involvement may include community activity, plant introduction or breeding, preservation of horticultural sites, teaching, research, extension and photography.

The Award

The award shall be cash in the amount of one thousand dollars ($1000.00) and a suitably inscribed plaque.

Nomination Process

Letters of nomination should include in-depth details with appropriate documentation of the candidate's achievements in horticulture. This will be the only source of information used to compare to other nominations.

All nominations must be received by May 31, 2010.

Nominations should be submitted to:
The Prairie Garden Awards Board
P.O. Box 517
Winnipeg, Manitoba   R3C 2J3

Announcement & Presentation

The recipient will be announced by September 1, 2010 with a presentation ceremony to follow as soon as practical thereafter. The winner will be featured in The 2011 Prairie Garden.

"The Prairie Garden" is an annual horticultural publication published by a group of volunteers for the furtherance of prairie horticulture.

Themes for The Prairie Garden Back Issues

We have back issues in varying quantities. Please use the form on the next page to order any of the following to complete your reference library.

2009 – Deciduous Shrubs *
2008 – Roses
2007 – The Edible Landscape
2006 – Myth, Magic & Meditation
2005 – Lilies
2004 – Pleasing Prairie Places *
2003 – Themes & Extremes
2002 – Landscape Design
2001 – Container Gardening
2000 – Herbs
1999 – Perennials *
1998 – Trees for The Prairies
1997 – Propagation
1996 – New Themes in Prairie Landscape
1995 – Accessible Gardening
1994 – Xeriscaping – Gardening in Dry Conditions *
1993 – Garden Herbs *Sold Out*
1992 – Garden Oddities
1991 – Sustainable Landscaping
1990 – Bulbs and Perennials *Sold Out*
1989 – 50 Years of Prairie Garden * *Sold Out*
1988 – Gardening Indoors
1987 – Perennials on The Prairies
1986 – New Ideas
1985 – Large Area Gardening *
1984 – Small Gardens *Sold Out*
1983 – Better Living Through Gardening
1982 – New Concepts, Gardening in Winter
1981 – Native Heritage
1980 – Mostly Trees and Shrubs *
1979 – Mostly Annuals *Sold Out*
1978 – Gardening Hints *Sold Out*
1977 – Flower Arranging *

* Issue contains an index of that year & previous 4 year's contents

The Prairie Garden
PO Box 517, Winnipeg, Manitoba R3C 2J3
Phone: (204) 489-3466; Fax: (204) 489-1644
Email: editor@theprairiegarden.ca / www.theprairiegarden.ca

❏ The 2010 Prairie Garden $12.00
Special quantity prices to horticulture societies and garden clubs:
10 – 49 copies $7.75; 50 – 149 copies $7.25
150 or more copies $6.75
Volume discounts to commercial outlets on request.

❏ Please add my name to the STANDING ORDER LIST in order that I
may receive a copy of *The Prairie Garden* every year starting with the
2011 issue. I will send my remittance upon receipt of each issue.
Standing Orders are charged at a discount rate.
(Do not check this box if your name is already on the Standing Order List)

BACK ISSUES (while quantities last) 2009:Deciduous Shrubs – $6.00
Previous issues (listed on page 183) prior to 2009
will be sold at $4.50 each while stock remains

POSTAGE AND HANDLING CHARGES APPLY ON ALL ORDERS
1 book – $2.95; 2-4 books – $10.25; 5-10 books – $17.25
11 books or more – Canada Post Weight Charges to apply
Postage will be charged at cost on all orders received from outside Canada.
All prices in Canadian dollars.
These prices supercede all previous price lists and are subject to change without notice.

Name			
Address			
City	Prov/State	P.C./Zip	
Qty	Year / Issue	Price Ea	Price
		Subtotal	
		Postage & Handling	
		TOTAL	

Please enclose cheque payable to:
"The Prairie Garden"